Tolerance
for Nonconformity

/\

A National Survey of
Americans' Changing Commitment
to Civil Liberties

Clyde Z. Nunn

Harry J. Crockett, Jr.

J. Allen Williams, Jr.

∧∧∧∧∧∧∧∧∧∧∧∧∧∧∧∧∧∧∧∧∧∧∧∧∧∧∧∧∧

Tolerance
for Nonconformity

/\

 Jossey-Bass Publishers
San Francisco • Washington • London • 1978

TOLERANCE FOR NONCONFORMITY
A National Survey of Americans' Changing Commitment to Civil Liberties
by Clyde Z. Nunn, Harry J. Crockett, Jr., and J. Allen Williams, Jr.

Library of Congress Catalogue Card Number LC 77-82920

International Standard Book Number ISBN 0-87589-362-7

Manufactured in the United States of America

JACKET DESIGN BY WILLI BAUM

FIRST EDITION

Code 7805

The Jossey-Bass
Social and
Behavioral Science Series

Preface

Citizens' tolerance for diversity is the core of the democratic process. The Bill of Rights specifies the extremes to which the government must go to avoid infringement on an individual citizen's liberties, but it also provides guidelines for citizens' relations to one another if democracy is to flourish. It is important, then, for the democratic society to understand how Americans are following the principles of the Bill of Rights, what forces are at work to further tolerance, and what can retard or destroy tolerance.

Tolerance for Nonconformity reports on a large-scale effort to provide information about these issues. A major national study of American commitment to civil libertarian principles has not been undertaken since Samuel Stouffer carried out his classic survey in 1954. Nearly two decades later, we set out to fill this research void by fielding a new study that relied on Stouffer's work as a baseline for changes. Closely following Stouffer, the new study included a large nationwide sample of American adults and a supplementary sample of community leaders. The information from these surveys shows how and why Americans have changed in their commitment to the principles of the Bill of Rights in the period between the McCarthy era and the Watergate era. Although the book is primarily designed for a professional audience, it is written so nonprofessionals can also understand what the study was about and what was found. For this reason, statistical details have been minimized.

The task of completing such a large-scale study is no simple matter. And even though differences among ourselves occasionally tested our own tolerance levels, complementary research interests provided a suitable division of labor. Clyde Nunn was primarily responsible for introductory and concluding discussions and for descriptions of attitude trends and the relationship of religion and tolerance. Harry Crockett concentrated his efforts on analyses of tolerance and the key demographic variables of education, age, place of residence, and gender. Allen Williams was primarily responsible for sections on issues of concern to Americans and on the relationship of social and political activism and tolerance for nonconformity. The three authors shared in the various tasks of the project and are solely responsible for the contents of this book.

The book is divided into eleven chapters. Chapter One presents a description of the background, purpose, and procedures of the study. Chapter Two focuses on what Americans worry about and what social issues concern them, giving special attention to how civil libertarian issues fit into their array of concerns.

Chapter Three narrows the focus to the changing state of support for civil liberties among citizens and community leaders. The various indicators of commitment to civil liberties are discussed and defended. Additional national data on tolerance for nonconformists supplement the two surveys in 1954 and 1973, giving us a reading on trends through 1977.

Chapter Four starts us on an extended effort to assess the social sources and dynamics of tolerance and the qualities that distinguish the tolerant and the intolerant. Education, the most powerful predictor of tolerance, is explored in this chapter. Chapter Five examines age and aging, important sociological variables closely associated with educational experiences, as well as the combined effects of age and education on attitudes toward civil liberties. After surveying these effects, the chapter attempts to anticipate their significance for the future.

The family and the school play an important part in the long-term process of learning tolerance, but the larger social context has an influence as well, as Chapter Six demonstrates. Size and heterogeneity of residential areas are rapidly changing in American society, and Chapter Six presents findings indicating that community size and regional context have become more important since 1954 in their effect on tolerance.

Chapter Seven looks at differences by sex in the support of civil liberties. The results of the analysis serve as a vivid reminder that what appears to be evident on the surface may not be true in fact, because our findings indicate that men are more tolerant than women in every category and that the greatest differences occur among those with the highest education. But this trend may be changing, and this change gives us a starting point for an explanation of these surprising findings.

Do religious Americans support individual freedom? Chapter Eight, in attempting to answer this question by investigating the relationship between religious affiliations, participation, and beliefs and the support of civil liberties, finds the impact of religion to be very strong.

Chapter Nine analyzes differences in tolerance between the public and those in positions of leadership. The main focus is on the structure of leadership and of democratic societies.

Chapter Ten attempts to uncover clues to the political roots of tolerance by examining the relationship of tolerance to interest in politics and current events, neighborhood opinion leadership, and sociopolitical participation. The relationship of citizen activism and civil liberties bears on at least two important questions: What are the social conditions for tolerance? And what are American attitudes toward tolerance likely to be in the future?

Finally, Chapter Eleven summarizes and synthesizes the study's findings in an effort to aid comprehension of where we have been in this study, where we might be going as a society with a less than overwhelming commitment to civil liberties, and how greater commitment might be facilitated.

No project of this scale can be carried out without the help of a number of people and organizations. Although the extent of assistance cannot be detailed here, we would like to acknowledge the contributions made by these people and agencies. In doing so, we stress that they are not responsible for the contents of this book. We thank the National Science Foundation for financial support of the project; the Center for Policy Research in New York and the Bureau of Sociological Research at the University of Nebraska for facilitating the project and providing valuable support from colleagues; Response Analysis, Inc. for expertly collecting the data for the 1973 study; the Inter-University Consortium for Political Research for use of Stouffer's 1954 study data; and the Newspaper Advertising Bureau for making final preparation of the manuscript less of a burden.

Special gratitude is due individuals who helped make the project possible and pleasant. We greatly appreciate suggestions for improving the manuscript from Amitai Etzioni, Nicholas Babchuk, Hugh Whitt, Richard Meile, Jack Seigman, Margaret Meinertz, and Susan Welch. Research and secretarial assistance was competently given by Louis St. Peter, Nora Cates, Patricia Moberg, Steve Crawford, Pamela Doty, Barbara Eckel, Dena Levy, Stephanie Goldman, Barbara Catandella, Myrna Stewart, and Mary Sheeran. Finally, Marsha Nunn, June Crockett, and Darlene Williams deserve our gratitude for help and patience throughout the entire project.

December 1977   CLYDE Z. NUNN
New York, New York
HARRY J. CROCKETT, JR.
Lincoln, Nebraska
J. ALLEN WILLIAMS, JR.
Lincoln, Nebraska

Contents

/\

xiii

The Authors

/\

CLYDE Z. NUNN is a senior research associate at the Center for Policy Research and senior project director at the Newspaper Advertising Bureau, New York City. He received his Ph.D. degree in sociology from the University of North Carolina, Chapel Hill, in 1964; his M.A. degree in sociology from the University of Louisville in 1960; Master of Religious Education degree from the Southern Baptist Theological Seminary in 1959; and B.A. degree from Furman University in 1957. He has taught at the University of Nebraska, Lincoln (1964–1972), and at Columbia University (1974–1977). Currently he is doing policy-related research in the areas of newspaper content and readership and public understanding of science and technology. Nunn's publications include *Achievement in American Society* (with B. C. Rosen and H. J. Crockett, Jr., 1969) and articles in *Daedalus, Social Forces, Journal of Social Psychology, Social Problems, Journal for Scientific Study of Religion,* and other journals and magazines.

HARRY J. CROCKETT, JR., is professor of sociology and psychology at the University of Nebraska, Lincoln. He received his Ph.D. degree in social psychology from the University of Michigan in 1961; M.A. degree from Washington University (St. Louis) in 1956; and B.A. degree from the University of Kansas in 1953. Crockett began his academic career at the University of North Carolina, Chapel Hill, where he was assistant professor of sociology (1960–1965). Since 1965, Crockett has taught at the University of Nebraska, Lincoln; he has also served as director of the Bureau of Sociological Research, is currently chairman of the Graduate Committee in Sociology, and is a member of the Executive Committee of the University of Nebraska Faculty Senate. He has frequently been a member of research review groups, including a four-year term with the Developmental Behavioral Sciences Study Section of the National Institutes of Health.

Crockett's books include *Achievement in American Society* (with B. C. Rosen and C. Z. Nunn, 1969) and *Achievement Among Minority Americans* (with J. L. Schulman, 1973). His continuing research interests are in social structure and personality and in socialization.

J. ALLEN WILLIAMS, JR., is professor of sociology at the University of Nebraska, Lincoln. He received his Ph.D. degree in sociology from the University of North Carolina, Chapel Hill, in 1963; M.A. degree in sociology from Cornell University in 1961; and A.B. degree from the University of North Carolina, Chapel Hill, in 1958. Before assuming his current position, Williams held positions at the University of Washington (1963–1965) and the University of Texas, Austin (1965–1968). He is a Phi Beta Kappa member and was a Woodrow Wilson Fellow. He has served as a member of the editorial board of the *Social Science Quarterly* since 1968. His areas of specialization are minorities, the sociology of the family, and social problems.

Williams has published several monographs and has research articles in such journals as the *American Sociological Review*, *Social Forces*, *Sociometry*, *Journal of Politics*, *Pacific Sociological Review*, *Social Science Quarterly*, *Public Opinion Quarterly*, and *Journal of Marriage and the Family*.

Tolerance for Nonconformity

/\.\.\.\/\.\.\.\/\.\.\.\/\.\.\.\/\.\.\.\/\.\.\.\/\.\.\.\/\.\.\.\/\.\.\.\/\.\.\.\/\.\.\.\/\.\.\.\/\.\.\.\/\.\.\.\/\.\.\.\/\.\.\.\

A National Survey of
Americans' Changing Commitment
to Civil Liberties

Chapter 1

Social Change
and Commitment to
Civil Liberties

/\\

Recent changes in the American people and their leaders form the basis for this focus on an important democratic attitude—tolerance—the willingness to grant civil liberties to fellow citizens, including those whose beliefs and opinions differ from society's mainstream.

Tolerance is a principle that the Bill of Rights established as a fundamental right of all Americans and one we like to believe is the backbone of our democracy. To find out how committed Americans are to this principle, over 4,000 Americans from all walks of life were asked nearly 200 different questions related to this subject. This book reports and analyzes their answers, revealing contemporary Americans' appreciation of some of the democratic rules-of-the-game, how they have changed in the last two decades, and what some of the sources and dynamics of attitudes toward civil liberties are.

This wealth of information gives us a clearer picture of where Americans—who are by no means monolithic—stand on civil liberties. Rank-and-file Americans and local leaders are becoming more willing to tolerate nonconformists. Changes in tolerance levels have occurred in every major social category. For example, women and men, old and young, educated and uneducated, have shown increases in tolerance, although some people changed more markedly than others. But perhaps the most important finding from our efforts to track trends in American tolerance is that citizens who are most supportive of civil liberties have emerged as the majority in our society—and they are not a "silent majority." In fact, those most willing to support civil liberties for nonconformists are among the most active and influential in their various communities. Finally, although trend is not destiny, and the study findings are not totally one-sided, there is rather sweeping evidence that social forces and modern institutions, especially education, are at work and are likely to generate even greater tolerance levels. These and other findings from the study receive detailed attention in the remainder of this book, but first let us view the study in a broad context and describe what we uncovered.

Social-Historical Context of the Study

Political culture does not evolve automatically or even uniformly. Accordingly, individual freedoms, although firmly documented by our nation's founding fathers, are in a process of change. At least two disrupting eras of American history, the McCarthy and Watergate eras, serve to remind us that full expression of civil liberties is neither inevitable nor immune to abuse by citizens or their government leaders. Historical, social, and economic forces shape both conceptions of and levels of commitment to civil liberties; consequently, we need to consider the social-historical context in which the civil liberties attitudes under investigation developed.

The so-called McCarthy and Watergate eras are referred to not only because they illustrate the point being made but also because they represent the historical bench marks for the present study. The baseline survey of our study was carried out in 1954, when the Army-McCarthy hearings were taking place and when Senator Joseph McCarthy was edging toward his precipitous decline in power and influence. The follow-up study was made in 1973, when Watergate was just beginning to be more fully revealed.

The post-World War II years were marked for change. When

the war ended, the world was left with the task of rebuilding. The first decade, according to historian Eric Goldman (1960), was a crucial one that set the tone for the years to come. The following decades saw unprecedented development and change in the United States and in much of the world. The Soviet Union let the world know that Communism was a force of no small magnitude and demonstrated her ability to compete with the United States as a world power. She flexed her technological muscle by exploding a nuclear device and successfully launching Sputnik. China quickly followed the Soviets as an emerging giant with her own version of Communism and technological sophistication, including a formidable nuclear capacity. The potential for worldwide nuclear holocaust was too frightening for most people to consciously admit very often, but it was—and still is— a potential nonetheless. The birth and growth of the United Nations during these post-World War II years moderated, but by no means dispelled, the anxiety. Wars between communist nations and the United States took the form of wars of containment, first in Korea and then in Vietnam. The Vietnam War had an especially devastating impact not only on Vietnam but on the United States as well. Among other things, it was an unsettling reminder to most Americans that the United States no longer reigned supreme in world affairs.

Just as the international situation changed dramatically in the post-World War II decades, so did the United States. Hungry for economic and social security, Americans became what John K. Galbraith (1958) labeled "the affluent society." American know-how was unleashed to accommodate the rapidly expanding demands for goods and services. Technological development during this period was no less than astonishing. Practically every arena of life felt the impact of this seemingly irreversible force. Medicine was revolutionized; faster and more extensive modes of transportation promoted mobility. The country—and the world—was shrunk by burgeoning and increasingly sophisticated communication technology. The computer became a necessity, if not a way of life. The quintessence of American scientific and technological advancement was the space program. Massive amounts of money and talent were concentrated on space exploration. The justification for the high national priority that the space program occupied has been challenged, but few would question that it was a technological achievement of the highest order (Etzioni, 1964).

Big corporations proliferated in numbers and power after World War II. By 1956, according to Samuel Eliot Morison (1972), 135 corporations owned 45 percent of all industrial assets in the United States. The extension of this power beyond national boundaries spawned multinational corporations and a host of political and moral issues. But big corporations were not restricted to industry. Big labor, big business, big government, and big education were parts of the increasingly organized and amalgamated society. It was the kind of corporate structure, according to Morison, that was designed to minimize the risks of free enterprise, and in doing so it redefined what security meant to Americans. In Morison's words (1972, p. 474): "The thrills of the old cutthroat wars between railway and steamship companies, and Standard Oil and its competitors, are now regarded as childish. From top executive to lowliest stevedores, everyone wants a steady job, producing predictable goods at a predictable cost, to be sold at a predictable price. That is what the country now means by security, not the guarantee of liberty that it meant in the eighteenth century."

The postwar years also brought dramatic demographic shifts to American society. Demographer Philip Hauser (1969) summarized these trends as population explosion, implosion, and diversification. These three population developments—increase, concentration, and greater heterogeneity—are closely linked with many of the changes discussed earlier and, as we shall see in the pages that follow, in large measure with changing civil liberties attitudes.

All these trends began before the 1950s and characterize countries other than the United States, but the United States has been one of the world's most dramatic examples of these demographic shifts. The magnitude of change, however, has accelerated since World War II. In 1950, the nation's population was well over 150 million. By 1960, the population total was 180 million; in 1970, it was over 203 million (U.S. Bureau of the Census, 1974). As for population concentration, the postwar years saw an acceleration of the trend toward an urban society: more than half of the U.S. population resided in rural areas until 1920 (Hauser, 1969); in 1950, 64 percent of the nation lived in urban areas; by 1970, 74 percent were city dwellers, and one out of every four citizens lived in or near one of the ten biggest urban areas (U.S. Bureau of the Census, 1974).

Diversification of the American population has come from multiple sources: foreign-born immigrants, internal migration, and population growth of various ethnic groups. In the early 1900s great waves of immigrants—over a million each year—came to this country. Then, between 1931 and 1945, the flow of immigrants subsided to about 35,000 per year. After World War II, greater numbers began coming again. In 1950, about a quarter million foreign-born persons arrived; in 1973, 400,000 new immigrants landed here. The number of natives of mixed or foreign parentage increased by almost a million between 1950 and 1960 and leveled off during the next decade (U.S. Bureau of the Census, 1974, 1975).

Along with population growth, concentration, and diversification, knowledge and sophistication levels were greatly expanding during the postwar years. Americans became exposed to extraordinary amounts of new and diverse information. The quantity of newsprint consumed between 1950 and 1972, for example, nearly doubled. Registration of copyrights (books, periodicals, music compositions, movies, and so on) increased from 210,564 in 1950 to 353,648 in 1973. The number of new books published more than doubled between 1955 and 1973. In 1955, 67 percent of American households had television; by 1970, 96 percent had television (U.S. Bureau of the Census, 1974, 1975).

Educational commitment and attainment also accelerated during the postwar period. Expenditures on education as a percentage of the Gross National Product are one indicator of a nation's commitment to education. Prior to World War II, expenditure for public elementary and secondary education was about 1 percent. In 1953–54, it was 2.5 percent; by 1967–68, it was estimated to be 3.8 percent. Expenditures for higher education took a sharp turn upward in the 1950s (Ferriss, 1969). Per-pupil expenditures, taking inflation into consideration, also reflect the elevated commitment to education during this period (Wattenberg, 1974). In 1950, Americans were spending $378 per pupil. In 1960, this figure was $546; in 1968, it was $828; and by 1972, it had risen to $1,026. Educational attainment also surged upward after World War II, as Chapter Four reports.

As immense and seemingly irreversible as these trends in American society were, the 1960s brought vivid reminders that the payoffs of "progress" were not thought to be equitably shared. Even the single-minded pursuit of consumer goods was beginning to be more vigorously challenged. Goldman (1960, pp. 345–346) described the dilemma confronting the nation as follows:

> Should the nation continue, in gradually altered form, the mood, the kind of leadership, the basic domestic and foreign policies that it had agreed upon in the Crucial Decade of 1945–55? Or did it need breakaways, genuine breakaways? Was it to be consolidation or innovation—more circumspect consolidation of the decisions of the Crucial Decade or venturesome innovation to a new kind of leadership, basically different ideas, a rethinking if not a redefinition of the whole national purpose? . . .
>
> For those who were certain that the United States would choose and hold to the path of genuine innovation, there was always history's yawning reminder. Fat and satisfied nations like America of 1960 have rarely been innovating societies. For those who were positive that the answer would be more consolidation, there were circumstances which even 5,000 years of history had never previously produced. . . . Having geared its life to endless upper mobility, it was endlessly subjected to the demands of millions for the better life in a constantly expanding definition of that phrase.

Rising expectations were not limited to the "haves." Symptoms of strain erupted in the 1960s. The black movement first followed the nonviolent lead of Martin Luther King, Jr., then became more militant. The omnipresent black movement marked the decade as a turning point in black demands for equality. Furthermore, its spirit seemed to spill over to other minority groups and to tap a rapidly rising social consciousness that was finding other expressions —in the ecology movement, the antiwar movement, and the women's liberation movement, to mention a few.

Some claimed the democratic pulse was beating a swift rate during the 1960s. Others spoke of a chaotic society, anarchy, and the demise of democracy. Whatever label is used, few would quarrel with the conclusion that the years after 1945, especially the 1960s, were times of staggering change, complexity, and uncertainty. The end of the Vietnam War, the energy crisis, a shaky economy, and Watergate altered the emphasis of the 1960s but not the temper of the times.

The transition of American society between the McCarthy and Watergate eras encourages a close look at changes in American commitment to the fundamental principles guiding our democracy. With the recent celebration of the nation's bicentennial, we need to appraise citizen commitment to those freedom-preserving principles embodied in the Bill of Rights. This period of history is especially important to study since it began and ended with concentrated attacks on citizens' civil liberties. Although the tactics of the Nixon era were more subtle than those employed by McCarthy, the Nixon administration abuses of civil liberties perhaps surpassed those of McCarthy. Not only was the White House violating civil liberties, the FBI, CIA, Army Intelligence, IRS, and other agencies had files on more than half a million citizens, illegally opened nearly a quarter million pieces of mail, monitored millions of telegrams and telephone calls, and used a variety of techniques to harass and defame private citizens. George Orwell's world of *1984* seemed dangerously at hand.

A healthy commitment to the principles of the Bill of Rights is becoming more important, not less. Our modern, complex society, with its diversity and its increasingly vocal citizenry, sets the stage for escalated conflicts and confrontations. The founding fathers of this country prescribed tolerance in the marketplace of freely flowing ideas as the key to the democratic process and the necessary condition for orderly change and innovation in a democratic society. We should carefully and periodically assess the American appetite for tolerance, our alertness to threats to civil liberties, and the conditions that strengthen or curtail that appetite.

Social-Psychological Context of the Study

From the social science point of view, the perspective from which this study views Americans, every society inevitably confronts the problem of how much individual freedom is possible and how much social control is needed. Obviously, if a human society is to persist very long, some balance of these needs is required. However, history has clearly shown that societies can vary widely from tightly controlled units to those that permit wide-ranging freedoms. Some societies die from excessive social controls; others eventually fail from anarchy or from too few or ineffective means by which the collective concerns of its members can be met. No one seems to know what the optimal balance is, but the more we learn about human groupings, the better able we are to specify both the conditions that produce the differences and the circumstances under which more or less social enforcement of controls is indicated.

One thing which the study of social science rather consistently shows is that most societies, large and small, have a strong tendency to tip the balance of social regulation versus personal freedom in the direction of the former. The inclination of societies—or at least of those people who effectively shape them—is to relinquish control begrudgingly, especially when strong winds of change blow with greater than usual force. Consequently, most societies stop short of knowing how much individual freedom can be tolerated before social cohesion is irreparably damaged.

In a democratically oriented society, the struggle between the forces of social control and individual freedom takes on a special quality. The nature of truly democratic societies is to maximize individual liberties and minimize the necessity of external, especially coercive, restraints. True democracies do not view the inevitable conflict of social constraints and personal freedom necessarily as a battle of two enemies. Instead, they are more properly accepted as leading to growth in both the social quality of life and individual fulfillment. Freedom in the democratic context carries the quality of a natural marriage of social and personal responsibility in an environment that offers access to a variety of options. Our Constitution and Bill of Rights are centrally concerned with structuring a society in which collective purposes can be pursued in an orderly and responsible manner and in which individual liberties can be maximized. The themes of restraint and checks-and-balances permeate these documents, but documents do not stand alone. Their legitimacy and viability derive from citizens. The restraints necessary to ensure collective accomplishments and individual freedoms must apply to individual citizens as well as to governmental and interinstitutional arrangements. Without individual restraint, individual freedoms quickly decay, and collective efforts disappear.

Although the ideal of democratic freedom seems fair and reasonable, the realities of American society tell us that at best we are in process toward that ideal. The American experiment first attempted to achieve democratization by the "melting pot" philosophy of homogenizing the variety and differences in our ranks. As early as the 1830s, a French observer of American democracy, Alexis de Tocqueville, warned of the "tyranny of the majority" and its pressures for conformity. It seemed like a simple matter of "Americanizing" everyone into a common mold; little did we know that the common mold was not so easily designed and that people were not so plastic. After two hundred years of our struggling as a democracy in a modernizing world, searching for a new formula to cope with persisting diversity and rising expectations, the indications are that differences among us will not disappear. In fact, the great diversity of our society, although causing us some anguish at present, may ultimately be our most important national resource.

Modern societies require modern people. Complex problems confront modern societies, and their resolution depends on high levels of rationality, planning, flexibility, sophistication, and openness. Societal structures must reflect these qualities, and individuals in the societies must acquire them as well. Tolerance seems well designed to fit the modern society. Inkeles and Smith (1974) selected the qualities of tolerance—openness to new experience, disposition to form or hold opinions, awareness of diverse attitudes and opinions, positive value placed on variations in opinions, and respect for the dignity of others—as components of their definition of modern individuals. Diversity of attitudes and opinions freely expressed is vital to modern democratic societies. Such societies must provide a supportive context for the development of these qualities.

In his earlier study of tolerance, Samuel Stouffer (1955, p. 220) concluded that there were "great social, economic, and technological forces" in American society that facilitated tolerance. He alluded to the modernization process that increasingly presents different values, ideas, and styles of behavior to people. Not only are people exposed to this greater variety, the modern context structurally imposes an interdependence that makes heterogeneous relationships nearly unavoidable. Such contacts often lead to greater tolerance as people realize that differences in other people are not so threatening as they first thought and that they must find a way to get along. This process is aided by the fact that members of complex societies typically have multiple roles and group affiliations that weaken the hold of more homogeneous group memberships. Blau (1974, p. 623) made the point concisely when he wrote: "People have wider circles of less intimate associates. The cocktail party is symbolic. The attenuation of profound social bonds that firmly integrate individuals in their communities is often deplored. But strong ingroup bonds restrain individual freedom and mobility, and they sustain rigidity and bigotry. Diverse intergroup relations, though not intimate, broaden horizons and promote tolerance, and they are the basis of macro-social integration."

Even the tasks—especially occupational—most frequently found in a modern, complex context appear to promote a willingness to expose oneself to new and different ideas. Kohn (1969) argued that people in middle-class occupations typically deal with manipulation of interpersonal relations, ideas, and symbols, whereas working-class occupations are more likely to involve manipulations of things. Middle-class people are therefore more likely than working-class people to value ideological diversity and to transmit this value to their children.

Other components of the modern context encourage tolerance of nonconformity, as we detail in subsequent chapters. No society—especially a modern one—leaves to chance the possibility that the broad social context alone will sufficiently call out of its members the kinds of attitudes and values deemed important. Institutions such as schools are set up to train people for the assumption of various roles in the society and to transmit skills, values, and attitudes for effective citizenship. Of course, institutions vary in their effectiveness in meeting these goals, and individuals differ in their levels of achievement. But as these skills, values, and attitudes become more widely recognized as important to the society, greater effort is likely to be made to make institutions more effective and to encompass a wider circle of people.

The learning of skills, values, and attitudes is not straightforward. It is complicated by immediate situational forces and by personality differences that stem from earlier training, especially in the family. People have unequal access to opportunities for learning and acquiring mainstream cultural skills, values, and attitudes. Indeed, one of the dilemmas of contemporary American society is how to correct maldistribution of opportunities and resources without compounding violations of rights and liberties.

Variations in social position also contribute to differences in personalities, which in turn have their own impacts on the learning process (see DiPalma and McClosky, 1970; Sniderman, 1975). Rokeach (1960), for example, observed that people with what he calls "open-minded" personalities are better able to evaluate information, regardless of its source, than people with "closed-minded" personalities. Personality is also directly involved in the nature of learning a particular attitude such as tolerance. For example, some people may learn to be tolerant because it is the prevailing norm; they adopt this norm to avoid negative sanctions for not doing so. Others learn that being tolerant brings certain positive rewards from other people who are important to them. Still others eventually integrate tolerance into their personal style, and the strength and persistence of the attitude depends on the personal value of the attitude and the ability to reward oneself for proper expression of the attitude. Kelman (1958) described these three processes of attitude change as compliancy, identification, and internalization. The same processes apply to learning intolerance as well. Kelman's description of attitude change is valuable when it allows us to view the same attitude in different people as having distinctive social-psychological bases, making the attitude more malleable in some people and less in others. Although the present study does not make these fine distinctions in tolerance attitudes, it does look for consistency and strength of commitment rather than relying on a single, amorphous indicator. More will be said in Chapter Three about what our indicators do attempt to measure, but meanwhile it is useful to define tolerance and how the present study employs the concept.

Definitions of tolerance abound, often with confusing effects. Tolerance is often equated with the lack of racial and ethnic prejudice. Although there is an overlap, tolerance as used in the present study is not the same as lack of prejudice. One may hold to prejudices and still be willing to let other people have their opinions and beliefs. Or one may even have a relatively benign attitude toward people of a particular ethnic background and yet frequently violate others' civil liberties.

Part of the confusion about what tolerance is derives from the equation of tolerance with acceptance. Acceptance is to agree with or condone the opinions, values, and behavior of others who are perhaps initially different from oneself. As it is understood here, the two are not the same. Tolerance is a straightforward attitude that allows people to have freedom of expression even though one may feel that their ideas are incorrect or even immoral. Such tolerance, however, does not condone free expression if it impinges on others' civil liberties.

Nor is tolerance merely a lack of social commitment or some passive acceptance of what exists because of a sense of powerlessness. Ideally it is an active process that reflects an appreciation of free-flowing diversity of ideas and the recognition that one's own free expression is made possible by such a climate of opinion. To be sure, ideals and practice do not totally mesh. Marcuse (1965) carried this observation one step further and argued that tolerance now stands as an inauthentic democratic privilege which in effect protects the advantage of the powerful by diluting policy criticism. Marcuse's argument is cogent but confuses the issue by equating tolerance of policies with tolerance of individual differences of opinion.

The tolerance that stems from the principles of the Bill of Rights should encourage an exchange of information and ideas that promotes rather than neutralizes policy evaluation. "Under the First Amendment," Justice Lewis F. Powell (*New York Times*, 1976a) wrote, "There is no such thing as a false idea. However pernicious an opinion may seem, we depend for its correction not on the consciences of judges and juries but on the competition of other ideas." We consider this the heart of tolerance. Here tolerance means the willingness to extend to others the right to express opinions and ideas that may be different. Other definitions of tolerance may be appropriate for other purposes, but here tolerance is defined in the simple terms of respect for others' civil liberties. (For a recent attempt to clarify the concept of tolerance, see Ferrar, 1976.)

Sources of the Study Information

Our information comes primarily from two nationwide surveys. The first study was done in the summer of 1954, at the height of Army-McCarthy hearings that later proved to be the end of the so-called McCarthy era in American politics. The second social survey was carried out in the spring of 1973, when the Watergate scandals were beginning to unfold but before the major events as we now know them became public. A third, independent data source was used to trace changes in tolerance of nonconformists and attitudes toward government wiretapping between 1972 and 1976. These nationwide data were collected by the National Opinion Research Center (NORC) of the University of Chicago. Several of the tolerance questions used in those surveys were taken from the 1954 survey, so that comparisons can be made with the 1954 and 1973 study results. The details of the 1973 survey will be described below, but first let us briefly describe the 1954 study that served as both the inspiration and model for our 1973 investigation.

Motivated mostly by the events of the McCarthy era, an eminent sociologist at Harvard University, the late Samuel A. Stouffer, designed and carried out the 1954 survey of rank-and-file Americans and community leaders. That study now stands as a classic in the survey research field, thanks to Stouffer's sensitivity to relevant social issues of his time, his keen analytical mind, and his nationally recognized skills in survey methods.

The details of how that study was done and its results are in *Communism, Conformity, and Civil Liberties: A Cross-Section of the Nation Speaks Its Mind* (Stouffer, 1955). Rather than recapping his book, we will describe in detail the 1973 study, since that survey was conducted, with a few exceptions, in an identical manner to that of Stouffer's 1954 survey. The following account of the 1973 survey notes where the two studies differ.

Personal interviews of about one hour's duration were used to obtain information from over 3,500 adult Americans (eighteen years old and over) and nearly 650 community leaders. An expert data collection agency, Response Analysis Corporation of Princeton, New Jersey, compiled the information.

The first priority of the 1973 survey was to ask many of the same questions that Stouffer asked in 1954. Because Stouffer was a leading survey researcher, his battery of questions met the highest research standards of his day. Indeed, he set some of the standards through his many contributions to social research methodology. Stouffer's expertise in designing the original questions made it possible to replicate his study with the assurance that any changes observed since his survey would reflect, as much as possible, new attitudes in the population, not variance caused by poorly worded questions, inadequate sampling, or generally weak methods.

Some of Stouffer's questions are inappropriate for today, and some questions used to measure certain characteristics in 1954 have been updated, drawing on advances in social science since Stouffer. Despite Stouffer's expert skills, there were areas, some of which he later recognized as important, that required newly developed indicators.

To measure tolerance of nonconformity, we relied on Stouffer's questions about Communists, Socialists, and atheists. Extending his description and explanation, we introduced new and modified areas of measurement, including tolerance of nonconformists such as demonstrators against a war like the one in Vietnam. In addition to Stouffer's questions about perceptions of threat, knowledge of Communists, reactions to violation of civil liberties, some psychological attributes, worries and concerns, and various background characteristics, our expanded measures included government wiretapping, threats from the political right, an expanded list of public worries and concerns, trust in leaders as well as people in general, and a greater variety of psychological indicators. An equally vigorous effort was made to improve the background characteristics that Stouffer claimed were important sources of tolerance. Stouffer used minimally adequate measures of religiosity, participation in voluntary associations, ethnicity, and occupational status. He had no measures of geographical mobility or occupational changes, both considered by Stouffer to be important sources of nonconformity tolerance levels.

After screening Stouffer's original questionnaire for useful items to include in the 1973 survey and adding new questions, we pretested the resulting questionnaire several times and made necessary modifications. Some 277 skilled interviewers were then trained for the specific requirements of the survey and sent to preselected locations around the country for personal interviews of 3,546 adults and 649 community leaders.

The interviewing began in late March 1973, and 82 percent of the total 3,546 general public interviews were completed within a month. Timing is important because interviewing that is drawn out risks not getting a cross section of a population at a given time. If an unexpected major event intervened between the time of the first and last interview assignments, it could seriously alter the responses of those last interviewed, which in turn could lead to serious problems in data interpretation. In relation to our 1973 survey, Watergate events were beginning to point to something greater than an every-day, take-it-for-granted government scandal; thus, we were concerned that these events might unevenly affect interviews completed at differ-ent times. After tabulating the completed interviews, we are consoled that the data show that the date of the interview made little difference in people's willingness to tolerate nonconformists. Of those inter-viewed during March, 55 percent were "more tolerant," compared to 53 percent interviewed in the first half of April, 54 percent of those interviewed in the second half of April, and 57 percent of those inter-viewed in May. The differences are not large enough to cause us to suspect that Watergate events during this time significantly affected responses to our measure of tolerance of nonconformists. The varia-tions observed here probably result from chance fluctuations rather than from any meaningful effect of the time of interview.

Precisely who was to be interviewed was determined by proba-bility sampling techniques used by the Response Analysis Corpora-tion. Typically, such techniques generate a sample that closely repre-sents the entire population. Existing data on characteristics of an entire population help to estimate how closely the sample compares with the population in distribution of these characteristics, such as age, education, sex, and ethnic background. A comparison of the sample and 1972 census figures on these characteristics revealed that the 1973 general public sample accurately reflected the national population. The differences between the survey sample and the cen-sus of the population were usually less than 4 percent, except for high school graduates, who were undersampled by 5.7 percent. Generally, however, the 1973 sample is a quite satisfactory reconstruction of the population on the characteristics listed above.

When a population is as vast and spread out as that in the United States, a set of explicit steps is necessary before the ultimate designation of the particular individual to be interviewed is made. The strategy is one in which selection moves from large population clusters to smaller units until an individual is specified. Simply outlined, sampling steps for the general public sample selection were as follows:

1. Based on the latest census information, the entire area of the coterminous United States was divided into Primary Sampling Units. These are well-defined geographic units, usually a county or a group of counties with a minimum population of 50,000 per unit.

2. From carefully specified population characteristics, 103 of these Primary Sampling Units were selected to be the pool from which 600 smaller population clusters were defined and randomly selected. These Secondary Sampling Units could be as small as a block or two in a densely populated area of a city, an entire county, or a larger sparsely populated rural area. Of the 600 Secondary Sampling Units or interviewing locations, 300 were randomly selected for use in the 1973 survey.

3. Each of the 300 Secondary Sampling Units was further divided into sampling segments, which typically included twenty-five to forty housing units. One or more segments were randomly selected from each of the 300 locations.

4. To ensure that all housing units were given an equal chance of being included in the sample, interviewers were instructed to personally list every housing unit in the segment. Without this procedure, units that no longer existed or that were added since published listings would bias the selection process.

5. After listing each housing unit, random selection by the Princeton central office produced the households where the interviewers would request permission to interview one adult. Advance letters to selected households introduced the study and the interviewers and requested participation in the study.

6. Finally, the specific adult to be interviewed was randomly selected after all adults currently living in the household were listed. Household members not living in the housing unit at the time were not included, so all members in hospitals or colleges were excluded. When only one adult was living in the household, that person was automatically interviewed.

This rather tedious but systematic sampling procedure was designed to ensure the greatest control possible over who was to be interviewed. Interviewers could not make substitutions, and extensive effort was made to track down the preselected individual to be interviewed. Typically, if the selected person was not available, four call-backs were made in attempts to reach the person.

Of course, some refusals occurred, and some people were unavailable. But steps were taken to increase the possibility that selected persons cooperated and that high-quality data were obtained. One important step was to use experienced interviewers thoroughly trained in the design, procedures, and interview schedule of the 1973 survey. Another step was to make an extraordinary number of call-backs to reach designated persons.

Complete success in reaching people and getting their cooperation in surveys has become increasingly difficult with their greater mobility and security consciousness. In our survey, completed interviews were obtained from 70 percent of the 5,077 eligible persons in the general public sample and 88 percent of the 736 eligible community leaders.

Stouffer's 1954 survey followed almost identical procedures and produced highly reliable survey data. One special procedure employed by Stouffer, but not by the 1973 survey, attests to the reliability of survey methods in general and his in particular. Instead of one national sample, Stouffer had two data collection agencies, the National Opinion Research Center and the American Institute of Public Opinion (Gallup Poll), collect data simultaneously from independently drawn samples. The results from the two samples were practically identical.

Even though those interviewed in 1954 were not the same persons interviewed in 1973, the procedures followed in both surveys give the next best thing to a study-restudy of the same individuals. If the 1954 and 1973 surveys adequately represent Americans at those specific times, changes in attitudes from 1954 to 1973 can be noted with considerable assurance that similar trends would be indicated had the entire population been interviewed.

The 1973 survey followed the 1954 study in still another way: A separate sample of local leaders was selected. And in both studies the same questions asked of rank-and-file Americans were asked of leaders. Samples of leaders were drawn in a slightly different manner from the sample of rank-and-file Americans. (Details on leader sampling, as well as other aspects of methodology, can be found in the Appendix.) In the 1973 survey of the general public, probability procedures were relied on up to the selection of the 300 Secondary Sampling Units, the sample locations. Since Stouffer's procedures were followed in defining the relevant sample locations as cities with populations between 10,000 and 150,000, the ninety-one cities that fit this definition were assigned interviewers. In the leader survey, a list of community and county leaders was adapted from an arbitrarily determined selection by Stouffer, with two exceptions. Stouffer included the following types of leaders in his study:

Mayor
Chairman of Community Chest
Chairman of board of education
Chairman of library committee
Chairman of Republican county committee
Chairman of Democratic county committee
Chairman of local American Legion post
President of county Bar Association
President of Chamber of Commerce
President of Parent-Teacher Association
Publisher of local newspaper
President of a large labor union local
President of the women's club
President of the local Daughters of the American Revolution (DAR) chapter

The 1973 study included all these leaders except the presidents of the local women's clubs and the presidents of the local DAR chapters. In their place, the presidents of the local Leagues of Women Voters and the city chiefs of police were substituted. The substitution was made on the grounds that the latter two leaders were more timely and significant than the two types included by Stouffer. In both studies the goal was not to be exhaustive in the choice but to include leaders at the community and county levels who were likely to be visibly respected, influential, or especially relevant to the studies (or all three). The ultimate purpose for studying leaders separately was to get a special appraisal of those individuals in the communities who were considered most likely to act on their opinions and to have the greatest influence in doing so. It is recognized, of course, that someone could devise a different but equally appropriate list of leaders. A new list including religious and minority community leaders is one example. However, to make comparisons with the 1954 study, some continuity of selection was necessary, and these leaders are on the whole important members of the community.

There is one qualification to note before comparing 1954 and 1973 leaders. When 1954 and 1973 comparisons are made, results will reflect deletion of the two leader types not included in both studies. Results of the responses of the two types of leaders included only in 1954 and the two types included only in 1973 will be reported here only when data are analyzed by each type of leader.

Some precautions should be taken when interpreting whom the 1973 leadership sample represents. As Stouffer warned in his study report, the leader sample is not a national cross-sectional sample in the same way the rank-and-file sample is. We cannot say from the sample of leaders that the answers they gave represent all leaders or even all local leaders. The sample of leaders, however, should represent the specified types of leaders who reside in municipalities with populations of 10,000 to 150,000; mayors, for example, represent all mayors of cities of the specified population. The city size, by the way, was established by Stouffer primarily to avoid the complications of combining such leaders as the mayor of, say, New York City with mayors of small towns. The 1973 study followed the same procedure because the principal intent in the study design was to make comparisons between the 1954 and 1973 findings.

Chapter 2

National Anxiety and Protection of Civil Liberties

/\.

During the early 1950s, public leaders repeatedly warned the American people of a Communist conspiracy to overthrow the United States government. The ultimate goal of Communism, the leaders said, was to control the world. Concern was expressed over the possibility of World War III, and Communists—both foreign and American—were said to be engaged in espionage and other subversive activities throughout the nation and the world. As Stouffer was collecting data for his study in the spring of 1954, the following headlines appeared in *The New York Times:* "Eisenhower Calls Red Peril Global and Truly Serious"; "Senate Warns World Reds to Stay Out of Americas"; "Dulles Doubtful on 'Co-Existence'"; "FBI Seizes 7 Men as Red Officials for Connecticut"; "End of Citizenship for Reds Voted."

One reaction to this threat was the attempt by government agencies, such as the FBI, to discover persons involved in activities that might endanger the society. Although many of these efforts were within the law and possibly necessary, some violated the civil liberties of citizens. Foremost among those persons apparently placing the discovery and exposure of Communists above the protection of constitutional rights was Senator Joseph McCarthy. People read about and watched on television his investigative hearings in which numerous accusations were made regarding suspected Communists and Communist sympathizers. The accused were from all walks of life, including some of the nation's most esteemed citizens: public officials, university professors, popular entertainers, scientists, news correspondents. Regardless of what McCarthy's personal motivations may have been, power or patriotism, the record clearly indicates that in the process of attempting to expose Communists, civil liberties were repeatedly ignored, careers and lives were ruined, and a climate of fear was created in at least some segments of the society's population (see Nevins, 1955; Lazarsfeld and Thielens, 1958).

The antidemocratic activities of McCarthy and other, less well known public figures during the 1950s may have been the most pervasive and devastating assault on constitutional liberties ever to have occurred in the United States, and yet several years passed before any effective counteraction took place. The lack of reaction gave the appearance of widespread public support, and it was this apparent support that most troubled civil libertarians. Why, they asked, would Americans approve of such flagrantly antidemocratic behavior? Maybe the public did not approve. Perhaps many were simply unaware of what was occurring. Given mass media coverage, however, a more likely possibility seemed to be that people may have been so afraid of Communism and world war that they were willing to sacrifice some of their constitutional rights under the assumption this would aid the society in its struggle against Communism. A victory against Communism, in turn, would enhance personal safety and national security. This proposition was largely responsible for prompting Stouffer to undertake his national study of attitudes toward civil liberties. In his words (1955, p. 13), a major purpose of the research was to examine "the reactions of Americans to two dangers. One, from the Communist conspiracy outside and inside the country. Two, from those who in thwarting the conspiracy would sacrifice some of the very liberties which the enemy would destroy."

Some Parallels Two Decades Later

Diplomatic talks in Peking and Washington, D.C., and movement toward detente with the Soviet Union may have eased tensions regarding Communism since Stouffer's study, but only a few years have passed since the nation extricated itself from the war in Vietnam. Concern has been renewed about the fate of the Republic of Korea (South Korea). The Arab-Israeli conflict is far from resolved. The arms race continues.

In addition to the concerns about Communism and global war, many other social issues have vied for attention in recent years. The United States population increased by 13 percent between 1960 and 1969, while the rate of serious crime, as defined by the FBI, increased by 148 percent; this increase in crime has continued into the 1970s (U.S. Department of Justice, annual). Population growth itself represents a problem of considerable concern. Largely due to the "baby boom" following World War II, the American population increased by 47 million people between 1940 and 1960. By 1970 the population was in excess of 203 million people, and according to the Commission on Population Growth and the American Future (1972), even with an average of two children per family the population will reach a size of over 350 million by the year 2070.

Environmental deterioration began to be recognized as a serious problem in the 1960s. In 1972, 29.3 percent of the nation's major watersheds were reported to be too polluted for designated uses, and at least half of the country had an atmosphere containing pollutants in excess of the government's primary or health standard. To add to environmental woes, declines in mineral reserves, especially petroleum and natural gas, culminated in an energy crisis beginning in 1972.

The largely nonviolent civil rights movement erupted into civil disturbances in the mid-1960s. Other groups began to openly profess their dissatisfaction with societal conditions. Student organizations made themselves heard, especially in opposition to the war in Vietnam. The National Organization for Women was founded in 1966. The Mexican American student walkout in Crystal City, Texas, which gave birth to the La Raza Unida Party, occurred in 1969. The

American Indian Movement began its occupation of Wounded Knee, South Dakota, in 1973.

Many other social problems that gained public attention in the past twenty years could be mentioned, such as poverty, inflation, and unemployment. However, this listing should suffice to make the point that a possible decline in concern about Communism does not necessarily lead to a corresponding decline in concern about national security and personal welfare.

In October, 1972, an editorial in *The New York Times* observed that "the President and his men have injected into national life a new and unwelcome element—fear of government repression, a fear reminiscent of that bred by the McCarthyism of twenty years ago. The freedom of the press, . . . the right to privacy, the right to petition and dissent, the right of law-abiding citizens to be free of surveillance, investigation and harassment—these and other liberties of the individual are visibly less secure in America today than they were four years ago" ("The Presidental Issue," 1972). Some of the events that led to this statement are still vivid in the minds of many Americans. For example, the civil disturbances that erupted in the nation's inner cities in the mid-1960s led the Secretary of Defense to create a Civil Disturbance Task Force under the direction of the Under Secretary of the Army. This task force in turn led to the creation of the Department of Army Civil Disturbance Information Collection Plan in 1968. It was classified Confidential. When this plan was declassified in 1971, it was revealed that the Department of the Army had been secretly spying on private citizens, collecting personal information about them, and storing this information in computer data banks. Ostensibly, the purpose was to gather information that would aid in the control of civil disturbances, but evidence indicated that the army had gone far beyond collecting data necessary for this function. According to Congressman Edward Koch (U.S., Congress, Senate, 1971), the army expanded its role to collecting information about anyone who might conceivably be unsympathetic to government policies. To some observers there was a serious question of whether the military had a legitimate right to secretly collect *any* personal information about private citizens.

The army's questionable behavior through its Civil Disturbance Information Collection Plan was not an isolated instance of violation of civil liberties. Aided by improvements in electronics and encouraged by some public officials, government surveillance of the public expanded greatly during the 1960s and early 1970s. And an unknown, but apparently large, proportion of the information collected was stored in permanent government files (U.S., Congress, Senate, 1971). Much of this information, such as data collected by the U.S. Bureau of the Census, was obtained in a perfectly legal manner and was necessary for the proper functioning of the government. Other information, however, was obtained or used in what seemed such flagrant violation of civil rights that the Senate Judiciary Subcommittee on Constitutional Rights held hearings on the subject of Federal Data Banks and the Bill of Rights. In his remarks before the Senate regarding these hearings, Senator Sam Ervin (U.S., Congress, Senate, 1971, pp. 235, 237) stated:

> It is not the carefully designed individual law enforcement data banks which concern the public. Rather, the subcommittee study is revealing that data programs which have aroused the most apprehension recently are those . . . which bear on the quality of first amendment freedoms by prying into those protected areas of an individual's personality, life, habits, beliefs, and legal activities which should be none of the business of government even in good causes. . . . When it is used to intimidate and to inhibit the individual in his freedom of movement, associations, or expressions of ideas, within the law, the new technology provides the means for the worst sort of tyranny. Those who so misuse it to augment their own power break faith with those founders of our Constitution who, like Thomas Jefferson, swore upon the altar of God eternal hostility against every form of tyranny over the mind of man.

Government surveillance and data storage typified a potential breakdown of the protection of civil liberties, a disregard by the very people sworn to uphold and protect them. Activities such as photographing people attending legal demonstrations and rallies, wiretapping public telephones, infiltrating legal organizations, and compiling dossiers on political activists without their knowledge did indeed seem to indicate the possibility of a new era of McCarthyism.

As we planned our study we knew that the 1960s had seen an

almost unprecedented legal strengthening of democratic principles. The 1962 Supreme Court decision declaring it unconstitutional to require children to recite prayers in school expressing a belief in God reaffirmed the principle of separation of church and state. The Civil Rights Act of 1964 established a federal right to equal opportunity in employment. The Voting Rights Act of 1965 eliminated many discriminatory practices in voter registration. In the 1965 case of *Miranda* v. *Arizona* the Supreme Court specified the permissible scope of police interrogation after arrests. A 1967 case, *Katz v. United States,* was essentially a reversal of the 1928 Olmstead case by the Court and held that wiretapping did constitute a "search" under the Fourth Amendment. The Civil Rights Act of 1968 included the provision that "all citizens of the United States shall have the same right, in every state and territory, as is enjoyed by white citizens thereof to inherit, purchase, lease, sell, hold and convey real and personal property." This support of democratic principles made the revelations of governmental violations of civil rights perhaps even more foreboding. Were we really moving into a new era of repression? We hoped our study would help answer this question.

During the months of data collection for the present study, reports of violations of constitutional liberties continued. Americans learned that the government had directed bombing of foreign nations without the public's knowledge and that illegal searches, especially in "drug raids," were frequent, almost commonplace. But by far the most disturbing events in the news at that time were those that can be combined under the general heading of the Watergate affair. Persons hired by the Republican Committee to Re-Elect the President were caught breaking into the Democratic National Headquarters in the Watergate building in Washington, D.C. Subsequent investigation exposed a wide range of illegal activities that not only had been encouraged but were participated in by high-level public officials, including the President of the United States. Illegal acts involved wiretaps, breaking and entering, perjury, misuse of campaign funds, misuse of federal agencies, obstruction of justice, extortion, and slander. Revelations in 1974 and 1975 regarding the FBI and CIA and the apparent complicity of the executive branch of the government suggest that violations of civil rights may have been more pervasive than had been imagined even after the exposure of the Watergate affair.

The Issue of National Security

As mentioned, Stouffer's concern in 1954 was whether Americans would be willing to sacrifice their civil liberties to protect the security of the nation. The same issue was of equal concern to us in the 1970s. There is no doubt that this is what some public officials were asking the people to do. For example, the following news release appeared in the Lincoln, Nebraska, *Sunday Journal and Star* on August 10, 1975, under the front page headline "Security Concerns Kelley": "Montreal (AP)—FBI Director Clarence M. Kelley said Saturday Americans must sacrifice 'a small measure of our liberties to preserve the great bulk of them' because of a growing threat to national security. . . . 'If investigative agencies charged with national security responsibilities are so fettered as to be ineffective—then we shall surely finish last in the world arena.' "

Perhaps there is a point where the general welfare conflicts with individual liberty, but using national security to justify suppression or violations of civil rights deeply disturbs some Americans. In the same news release just cited, Albert Jenner, former minority counsel to the House Judiciary Committee's impeachment panel, said that Kelley wants the FBI to have the right to judge "what is in the so-called national interest and under this guise use whatever methods, regardless of the Constitution. I absolutely disagree with his statement that we must give up some rights in the interests of national security, because when you surrender even a small measure of your liberties you then accept the inevitable destruction of what remains."

How have people reacted to these statements and events? Are they, as was suggested in *The New York Times* editorial quoted above, living in a climate of fear brought about by governmental suppression of individual liberties? Or are they so afraid for their safety and for the security of the nation that they welcome these violations? Both scholars and popular writers have suggested that the latter view is true. However, as might be imagined, some view this reaction positively, while others are troubled. Among those responding favorably, Inbau and Carrington (1971, p. 23) provide a good example: "This is the voice of the majority—the law-abiding majority—a group which now demands a hard line on crime and which is clearly willing to turn away from the contrived rights of the criminal in order to vindicate the overriding right of every citizen: the right to be safe." On the negative side, Hentoff (1973, p. 156) commented: "Why do we stand by as our privacy is raped? Why do we acquiesce as the rapidly growing quantity of information being fed to and distributed by the FBI data bank threatens to become what Senator Charles Mathias, a liberal Republican from Maryland, calls 'the raw materials of tyranny'? Part of the answer is fear: a national fear, born in the late Sixties, of demonstrators, of blacks, of students, of muggers. The national desire, an almost desperate desire . . . is for order. In this kind of climate, the majority of the people are much more concerned with their safety than with civil liberties."

In following chapters we shall examine the origins of support for democratic principles: the effect of formal education, of being male or female in our society, of living in a city or on a farm, of living in one region of the nation or another, of being old or young, of being a civic leader or a member of the rank and file. All these factors help us understand how our society functions and what the future is likely to be. Here we will focus on the questions that prompted the original research by Stouffer and our own study. Are Americans so fearful for their safety that they are willing to forgo their constitutional liberties or the liberties of their fellow citizens? Have governmental repressions or violations of civil liberties made people afraid or reluctant to exercise their rights?

Is There a National Anxiety Neurosis?

Let us begin by examining how optimistic people are about their futures, how much they worry, and what they say they worry about. After obtaining information necessary for the selection of the proper respondent in each of the randomly selected households throughout the nation, the interviewers asked, *"On the whole, do you think life will be better for you or worse in the next few years than it is now?"* The responses obtained by Stouffer and by the present study are shown in Table 1. Perhaps the population has become slightly more polarized, since there are higher percentages answering "better" and "worse" in 1973. But the major finding is that a majority say their lives will improve. From the 1954 findings Stouffer (1955, p. 59) concluded that the American people were generally optimistic: "the most striking fact was the essential optimism in the American

Table 1. Optimism About the Future, 1954 and 1973.

| | 1954 | | 1973 | |
Response	Percent	Number	Percent	Number
Life will be better	57	2,828	61	2,153
Life will be about the same	23	1,100	19	683
Life will be worse	13	658	16	580
Don't know	7	346	4	130
Total	100	4,932	100	3,546

climate. Only 13 percent said they expected life to be worse for them in the next few years than it is now—an answer which is hardly compatible with an overwhelming concern with impending doom." There is no reason to discount this interpretation. Fifty-seven percent of the people in 1954 and 61 percent in 1973 did indicate their lives would be better, and older people were disproportionately represented among those believing their lives would be worse. However, a word of caution should be introduced since we do not know how many of those saying life will be about the same were unhappy with their situation, nor do we know why some people did not want to answer the question.

Our next question probed more directly into personal worry or anxiety. Respondents were asked, *"Everybody, of course, has some things he worries about, more or less. Would you say you worry more now than you used to, or not as much?"* Both in 1954 and in 1973, more than one in three said they never worry or do not worry as much (37 and 36 percent respectively), but almost half said they worry more now (45 and 47 percent). On first impression this finding would appear to represent a rather sharp rise in anxiety during both time periods. However, we have no way of determining whether the percentages are larger than they might be in more tranquil times.

After answering the previous question, respondents were asked, *"What kinds of things do you worry about most?"* Table 2 shows the percentage distribution for the first response and the first three responses. The first response of a majority of respondents—69 percent—concerned their families or themselves. Eighteen percent specifically mentioned being worried about a social issue on their first response. Additional computation shows that 39 percent voiced a

Table 2. Spontaneously Expressed Worries, 1973.

Type of Worry	First Response Only (Percent)[a]	First Three Responses (Percent)[b]
Family problems		
Financial	19	30
Health (self or family)	15	27
Other	19	30
Personal problems		
Job, financial	1	3
Job, other than financial	7	12
Other	8	13
Social problems		
Inflation (high prices or taxes)	8	22
Crime	2	6
Drugs	1	7
Pollution	0	2
Other	7	20
All other problems	2	6
Don't worry, don't know, or no second or third response	10	70

[a] Percentages are based on the 3,546 respondents constituting the total sample.

[b] Percentages using first, second, and third responses add up to more than 100 percent, since there are more responses than cases.

worry about a social problem at least once among their first three responses. Many different social problems were mentioned, but inflation, crime, drugs, and pollution were the most frequently cited.

On the basis of answers to these questions, a substantial proportion of the American population appears to be relatively calm: 61 percent of the people said their lives will improve in the next few years; 52 percent said they worry no more than previously, worry less now than they used to, or never worry; and, although most people admitted to having some worries, 61 percent made no mention of being concerned about a national or world problem. Thus, the society does not seem to be in a state of panic or fear; we find no national anxiety neurosis or overwhelming concern with impending doom. On the other hand, it also is possible that the response patterns reflect an undercurrent of concern—not fear, but something more closely akin to malaise or apprehension. Thirty-nine percent do not think their lives will improve soon, and 47 percent said they worry more now. Given the salience of one's own personal affairs, it may be very significant that as much as 39 percent of the people mentioned a national or world problem among their first three responses when asked what they worry about most.

Cantril and Roll (1971) made what may prove to be a very astute observation. They suggested that it is possible for people to have a sense of optimism about their own lives and future while being deeply troubled about conditions in their society. This can occur, they said, when serious social and political problems are just beginning to force their way into people's lives (p. 52): "Although people are apprehensive about what they see going on around them, they cannot be characterized as distressed, confused, or groping when it comes to their individual lives. . . . The topics at issue have not, as yet, impinged sufficiently upon the individual's daily routine and well-being to preclude his enjoyment of the good life." The social and political problems that Cantril and Roll mentioned specifically are inflation, drugs, pollution, crime, and political instability. Let us examine what people said when asked about these and similar problems.

In the 1954 and 1973 surveys interviewers read the following statement to each respondent, *"Here is a list of topics which have been discussed in the papers recently. Which ones do you remember talking about with your friends or relatives in the last few weeks or so?"* Each respondent was then handed a card that included Communists in the United States, crime, danger of World War III, high prices, high taxes, and racial problems. A comparison of responses for the two time periods showed a sharp decline of interest in Communists (35 to 16 percent) and the danger of World War III (35 to 12 percent). Interest in racial problems remained about the same (36 and 37 percent), and there was greatly increased concern with crime (37 to 59 percent), high prices (52 to 88 percent), and high taxes (26 to 62 percent).

The 1973 survey included a number of additional topics, and

for each respondents were asked, *"Do you think it represents a serious or moderate threat to the United States, or is not a threat to the United States?"* The responses presented in Table 3 show that in addition to

Table 3. Public Perceptions of the Seriousness of
Selected Social Problems, 1973.

	Percentage answering:			
Selected Problems	*Serious Threat*	*Moderate Threat*	*Not a Threat*	*Don't Know*
Drugs	78	15	4	3
Crime	75	19	3	3
High prices	75	18	5	2
High taxes	58	27	9	6
Pollution	51	31	11	7
Juvenile delinquency	39	38	16	7
Poverty in the United States	39	36	17	8
Racial problems	33	43	17	7
Communists in the United States	29	33	26	13
Urban problems	25	36	23	16
Population increase	22	35	34	9
Hippies	15	26	51	8
Danger of World War III	14	35	37	13
Radical college students	10	32	46	12
Revolution	10	29	48	14
Right-wing groups	8	27	45	20
Women's liberation	6	18	65	11

Note: Percentages are based on 3,546 cases.

crime and inflation, over half the adult population would include drugs and pollution as serious threats to the society. Among the issues listed, only women's liberation and hippies are perceived as not representing a threat by a majority of respondents.

Another public concern mentioned by Cantril and Roll is political instability. In our survey respondents were asked, *"In general, how much trust and confidence do you have in the wisdom of state and community leaders when it comes to making political decisions?"* The same question was repeated in reference to national leaders. A majority, 52 percent, said they have a good deal of trust in state and community leaders, and another 8 percent said they have a very great deal of trust in them. However, 33 percent said they have "not much" trust, and 4 percent said they have no trust at all in these leaders. Attitudes toward national leaders are slightly more positive, but one third indicate having little or no trust and confidence in them. Since we do not have measures from previous time periods, we cannot conclude that these findings represent a breakdown in public trust in leaders. Nevertheless, it is clear that a sizable minority of Americans are less than confident in the ability of public officials to make sound political decisions.

The evidence appears to support the contention that people can be personally optimistic while being troubled about societal conditions. The issues of most concern to Stouffer in 1954, Communism and global war, have receded in importance—at least a much smaller percentage of people talk about them with friends and relatives. But other issues—drug abuse, crime, inflation, pollution, juvenile delinquency, poverty, and racial problems—have taken their place. In addition, about one in three persons said they have little or no trust and confidence in state, community, and national leaders.

Concern About Civil Liberties

Is the public concerned with violations of constitutional liberties perpetrated by government representatives? In fact, are people even aware that their liberties are threatened? Let us begin with the second question.

Respondents were asked: *"Which of these views is closest to your own?"* They were then handed a card that listed the following choices: *All people in this country feel as free to say what they think as they used to; Some people do not feel as free to say what they think as they used to; Hardly anybody feels as free to say what he thinks as he used to.* Fifty-five percent chose the first response, and 33 percent chose the second. Two percent had no opinion, leaving only 10 percent perceiving extreme threat to free speech. Nevertheless, the finding that one third of the national cross section think some people do not feel as free to say what they think as they used to suggests that many people believe repression is occurring. The percentages are scarcely different from those obtained by Stouffer during the McCarthy era. He found 31 percent answering "some people" and 10 percent answering "hardly anybody feels as free to say what he thinks as he used to."

Following this question, respondents were asked, *"What about you personally? Do you or don't you feel as free to speak your mind as you used to?"* A smaller percentage thought their own right to free speech was threatened. Twenty percent said they felt less free than before, and 2 percent were not sure, leaving 78 percent saying they feel as free as ever to speak their minds. It is interesting to note, however, that 87 percent felt this way in 1954.

Turning to the question of whether people are concerned about violations of civil liberties, recall that 39 percent of the public mentioned a social problem when asked what they worried about most. However, less than 1 percent mentioned being worried about invasions against constitutional rights. When we asked people about a specific instance of potential violation of their liberties (the military keeping files on private citizens), 15 percent said this posed a serious threat to the nation, and another 26 percent said it represented a moderate threat. Apparently a number of people either had mixed feelings or were unfamiliar with this action by the military since 23 percent said they did not know whether this was a threat or not. Nevertheless, 41 percent indicating this action represents a threat to the United States suggests that a considerable number of people are concerned about their civil rights, even if this subject is not uppermost among their worries.

A Reinterpretation of Stouffer's Conclusions About a National Anxiety Neurosis

Certain public leaders and other citizens have advocated the repression and violation of civil liberties as being necessary to help solve some of the nation's problems. The military has argued that surveillance of private citizens and keeping files on their personal lives were necessary to prevent civil disturbances. FBI surveillance of civil rights leaders has been justified on similar grounds. Many of the activities associated with the Watergate affair were said to be necessary for the protection of national security. It has been argued that the Miranda rule and other regulations protecting due process of law should be abolished because they inhibit the police and thus endanger the law-abiding population. In light of events such as these, the present study raised questions similar to those asked by Stouffer: "Are Americans so fearful for their safety they are willing to forgo their constitutional liberties or the rights of their fellow citizens?" and "Have governmental repressions or violations of civil liberties made people afraid or reluctant to exercise their rights?"

Stouffer found a majority optimistic about the future, a finding seemingly inconsistent with the idea of a national anxiety neurosis. When people were asked what kinds of things they worried about, most mentioned personal and family problems, not social issues. When he probed more directly about social problems, the percentage indicating concern increased, but even this procedure found what appeared to be limited anxiety. Based on these findings, Stouffer (1955, p. 87) concluded that "the threat of future war can stir apprehension in the breasts of parents of children of any age—although surprisingly few parents or other adults in our sample put war high on their list of worries. The internal Communist threat, perhaps like the threat of organized crime, is not directly felt as personal. It is something one reads about and talks about and even sometimes gets angry about. But a picture of the average American as a person with the jitters, trembling lest he find a Red under the bed, is clearly nonsense."

The comparable findings in our study do not differ greatly from Stouffer's, but our interpretation of their meaning does vary somewhat. As in the original study, we found a majority optimistic about the future and a majority worried about family and personal rather than social problems. These findings do not suggest widespread anxiety to us any more than they did to Stouffer. However, two additional points should be considered. First, by emphasizing the responses of the majority, it is possible to overlook the significance of the minority responses. Second, it is possible for people to be deeply troubled about social issues yet still optimistic or satisfied with their own lives. Let us consider these points in reference to what people told us about social problems.

When people were asked whether certain issues threatened the United States, the results indicated considerable concern, especially about drugs, crime, high prices, high taxes, and pollution. A majority told us that these problems are serious threats to the country. Additionally, 39 percent said juvenile delinquency and poverty are serious threats, and one third said the same thing about racial problems. Even a problem of apparently declining concern, Communists in the United States, produced a response of "It's a serious threat" from 29 percent. Twenty-nine percent is a minority opinion, but it is the opinion of more than one of every four adult Americans—millions of people.

With respect to attitudes about public leaders, a majority indicated trust and confidence in them. However, once again, perhaps we should pay attention to the possible importance of the minority view. Only 4 percent said they have no trust at all in the wisdom of public officials, but 33 percent said they do not have much trust or confidence in state and community leaders, and 29 percent said they feel the same way about national leaders. What are the implications for the country when about one third of the adult population has little confidence in public leadership? Combined with the findings regarding social problems, this finding suggests to us that a very large number of Americans are concerned about the state of their nation. We do not believe there is a national anxiety neurosis, no fear of "Reds under the bed" or of hippies and drug addicts similarly located, but we do believe that millions are apprehensive about societal conditions.

An important objective of both the original study and this one was to discover how people felt about violations of their civil liberties. Neither the question about worries nor our primary example of recent invasions of rights by the military elicited as great a show of concern as did many of the other social problems. However, when respondents were asked about possible repression of civil rights in a more general way—whether people feel as free to say what they think as they used to—33 percent said that some people felt less free and another 10 percent said that hardly anybody felt as free as they used to. Twenty percent said their own freedom of speech was less secure. Our assessment of the meaning of these findings is that Americans are less concerned about, or at least less aware of, threats to their rights than about a number of other issues, but substantial minorities show evidence of apprehension or malaise. Nearly half felt that some repression of free speech was occurring, and 20 percent thought it was happening to them.

Chapter *3*

Changing Commitment
to Civil Liberties

ᐱᐱᐱᐱᐱᐱᐱᐱᐱᐱᐱᐱᐱᐱᐱᐱᐱᐱᐱᐱᐱᐱᐱᐱᐱᐱᐱᐱᐱᐱᐱ

The American bicentennial provided an opportunity to celebrate the political ideals of this country. The symbols of the Great American Experiment, the Constitution, the Bill of Rights, the Statue of Liberty, and hundreds of others were paraded for Americans and the rest of the world to review. Pride in the rich diversity within the United States was proclaimed. Tolerance of differences was hailed.

Celebration of ideals is important for a nation, but ideals are guideposts, not actualities, and sooner or later reality testing takes place. Actual commitments to Bill of Rights' principles are forged on the hard anvil of human exchange, so full accomplishment of civil liberties seems always to be in process, not a reality that is established and irreversible.

The legal structure of a society has a great deal to do with the realization of individual liberties, but in a democratic society, the legitimacy of and support for civil libertarian principles also derive from citizens, albeit more from some segments of the citizenry than others. Political principles without a social base are coercive. Lofty ideals without citizen commitment are only illusions.

If in fact Bill of Rights' principles are important, and if their realization is a developmental process that depends in a significant way on more than public indifference, it is important to periodically take a reading of the pulse of American commitment to civil liberties principles.

Both Stouffer's 1954 survey and our 1973 survey were designed to minimize question bias in such a politically sacred area as commitment to the principles of the Bill of Rights. If asked about broad, abstract principles, the great majority of citizens appeared to support these principles (Prothro and Grigg, 1960). On the other hand, if specific and concrete questions were asked, greater variation was noted. The less abstract questions were asked in both the 1954 and the 1973 surveys. However, even specific questions are not problem free. This issue and other questions about the validity of the data will be taken up again later in the discussion. Meantime, let us look at the evidence that Americans are changing in their commitment to principles outlined in the Bill of Rights.

One way to approach the problem of politically sensitive opinions is to force a choice between two alternatives that include clear-cut trade-offs between moral principle and pragmatic concerns. For example, in 1954 and 1973 respondents were asked whether it was more important "to find out all the Communists even if some innocent people should be hurt" *or* "to protect the rights of innocent people, even if some Communists are not found out."

The shift in responses to that choice from 1954 to 1973 was dramatic, as seen in Table 4. In 1954 the majority (58 percent) of citizens were more likely to prefer finding out all Communists than protecting the rights of the innocent. Although community leaders in

Table 4. Importance of Protecting Rights of Innocent, 1954 and 1973.

	Percent Answering:			
Sample	*Find Out Communists*	*Don't Know*	*Protect Innocent*	*Number*
1954				
Community leaders	42	6	52	1,500
National cross section	58	10	32	4,932
1973				
Community leaders	11	2	87	648
National cross section	23	7	70	3,543

1954 and 1973 were more likely than the national cross section to emphasize protection of the innocent, 70 percent of the general public in 1973 also said that the innocent should be protected even if some Communists go undetected—an enormous increase over the 32 percent of the 1954 general public sample who elected to protect the innocent.

Since the strains of the McCarthyism of the 1950s, Americans probably feel that they have learned something about tolerance of those who hold views which are not accepted by a majority. It will come as no surprise then that Americans, both the cross section of the nation and those who hold special civic responsibilities, have become more tolerant of Communists, Socialists, and atheists. It might be a considerable surprise to many, however, to learn that so many in 1973 would allow an admitted Communist, an admitted Socialist, and an admitted atheist to make a speech in their communities or to teach in a college.

Let us consider tolerance for a Socialist first. In 1954 and 1973 a cross-sectional and a leadership sample were asked: *"If a person wanted to make a speech in your community favoring government ownership of all the railroads and big industries, should he be allowed to speak?"* Table 5 gives the responses to the question. In 1954, 84 percent of the leaders and 58 percent of the national cross section were willing to let a Socialist speak. By 1973, 91 percent of the leaders and 72 percent of the general public were tolerant of a Socialist's right to speak.

Should such a person be allowed to teach in a college or university? A majority of the 1973 cross section and community leaders

Table 5. Tolerance for a Socialist's Freedom of Speech, 1954 and 1973.

| | Percent Answering: | | | |
Sample	No	No Opinion	Yes	Number
1954				
Community leaders	14	2	84	1,500
National cross section	31	11	58	4,933
1973				
Community leaders	8	1	91	649
National cross section	21	7	72	3,538

Table 6. Tolerance for a Socialist's Right to Teach, 1954 and 1973.

| | | Percent Answering: | | |
Sample	No	No Opinion	Yes	Number
1954				
Community leaders	47	5	48	1,500
National cross section	54	13	33	4,933
1973				
Community leaders	26	6	68	647
National cross section	38	9	53	3,539

supported academic freedom for Socialists, but they were more restrictive on civil liberties in academic settings than on freedom of speech in the community at large (Table 6). A third of the public and nearly one half of the leaders in 1954 were willing to let a Socialist teach in a college. In 1973 over two thirds of the leaders and half of the public gave tolerant responses. Again, leaders in 1954 and 1973 were more tolerant than the cross section of Americans, but both groups became more tolerant on this issue in 1973.

So far all leaders have been combined in reporting results. There is, however, reason to wonder whether different types of leaders, public officials or commanders of the American Legion, for example, might not vary in tolerance levels among themselves and in comparison to rank-and-file citizens. Table 7 gives the percentage willing to let a Socialist speak in their communities for each leader category as well as the percentage of the cross section willing to do so.

Without exception, regardless of the particular area of civic responsibility of leaders, local leaders in 1954 and 1973 were more willing than the public to let a Socialist speak in their communities. Of all leader categories, only the presidents of local labor unions in 1973 came close to the national cross section in the percentage tolerant of Socialists. Labor union presidents, along with local Democratic party chairmen and chairmen of the Community Chest, were also the only leaders for whom there were comparable data that failed to show an increase in tolerance since 1954.

When the leaders and the general public were asked questions about civil liberties for persons who represented a clear-cut ideological deviancy for many Americans—atheists—response patterns similar

Table 7. Tolerance of a Socialist's Freedom of Speech, by Type of Leader, 1954 and 1973.

Type of Leader	Percent Willing to Let a Socialist Speak in Their Community:	
	1954	1973
Public officials		
Mayors	80	98
Presidents, school board	88	94
Presidents, library board	92	96
Police chiefs	—	98
Political party chairmen		
Republican county central committee	87	92
Democratic county central committee	91	84
Industrial leaders		
Presidents, Chamber of Commerce	85	88
Presidents, labor union	80	73
Heads of special patriotic groups		
Commanders, American Legion	76	78
Regents, DAR	75	—
Others		
Chairmen, Community Chest	93	90
Presidents, bar association	95	100
Newspaper publishers	97	98
Presidents, women's club	68	—
Presidents, League of Women Voters	—	96
Presidents, Parent-Teacher Associations	79	94
Average of community leaders	84	91
National cross section	58	72

to those found in regard to Socialists emerged. Religion persists as a pervasive concern among Americans, a fact that is documented in Chapter Eight. Not surprisingly, then, we found Americans generally more tolerant of Socialists than of atheists.

A majority of leaders in both surveys gave an atheist the right to make a speech in their community: 64 percent in 1954 and 87 percent in 1973. Approximately a third (37 percent) of the public in 1954 gave the tolerant response toward atheists, but that percentage increased to nearly two thirds (62 percent) by 1973.

Support for academic freedom for atheists is another matter. Like the Socialist, the atheist is much less tolerable to Americans when it is a question of permitting such a person to be a college professor. A majority of rank-and-file Americans still feel that what is taught in our colleges and universities should be closely guarded, at least when the question of whether or not to allow someone who does not believe in God to teach is raised: in 1954 only 12 percent and in 1973 only 39 percent agreed that an atheist teacher had the right to hold that job. Thus, although a majority of the American public do not favor censoring someone making a speech against religion, they apparently consider the college campus, the acclaimed citadel of free exchange of ideas, an inappropriate place for an atheist, even though the question does not suggest that atheism would be the subject of his teaching. The majority of leaders in 1973—59 percent—were more consistently tolerant toward Socialists and atheists, but in 1954 only a small percentage of leaders—25 percent—would allow an atheist to teach.

Clearly, atheists are less tolerable to Americans than Socialists. Even among leaders, libertarian responses were less evident toward atheists than toward Socialists. Nevertheless, all types of leaders, except 1973 commanders of American Legion posts, were more willing than the national cross section to let atheists speak in their communities, and all types of leaders have become more tolerant of atheist speechmakers since 1954.

Atheists represent a more stringent test of American tolerance than Socialists, but despite the ebbing of the cold war, Communists remain America's number one ideological enemy. Even though only 18 percent reported ever having known a Communist in 1973, for example, 65 percent of the 1973 sample believed that internal Communism was a serious or moderate threat. This finding does not necessarily suggest that the Communist threat is simply a consequence of public ignorance and fantasy; it reflects both the reality of the threat of war with the Soviet Union and the formless quality of Americans' conceptions of Communists. For these reasons, questions about Communists provide a vigorous test of American tolerance.

If a person who admits to being a Communist wanted to make a speech in a community in 1954, Stouffer's data clearly indicate that he would not have gotten very far with the typical community member. However, if the same Communist made a similar attempt today, the 1973 study results indicate that his troubles would be less severe, even though it would not be exactly smooth sailing, with 41 percent of the rank-and-file citizens unwilling to let him speak. However, with local leaders' strong support of freedom of speech in 1973 (78 percent versus 51 percent in 1954) and the bare majority of citizens (53 percent in 1973 versus 27 percent in 1954) willing to allow a speech by a Communist, the climate of the American community has changed sufficiently to accommodate the situation. Both leaders and the general public have increased their tolerance of nonconformists, but leaders continue to be more willing than the rank and file to give a Communist the right to speak.

When the same question is considered for specific types of leaders, attitudes of leaders toward Communists are, with few exceptions, distinctly libertarian. Only local labor union leaders and commanders of American Legion posts fell below the national cross-sectional norm in 1973. In 1954 all types of leaders were more willing than the national cross section to allow a Communist to speak.

Leaders and national cross sections in 1954 and 1973 were also asked in specific terms about freedom of the press: *"Suppose he [an admitted Communist] wrote a book which is in your public library. Somebody in your community suggests the book should be removed from the library. Would you favor removing it?"* Responses to this question were similar to those to the previous question about free speech for admitted Communists. Again, a majority of leaders and the general public in 1973 were tolerant of admitted Communists: 79 percent of the civic leaders and 54 percent of the citizens would not favor removal of a book written by a Communist. These results represented considerable advancement in tolerance since 1954, when only 42 percent of the leaders and 27 percent of the citizens would grant freedom of the press to admitted Communists.

What about people who are suspected of being Communists but who deny it? Does the Communist tag carry such weight that one needs only to be labeled "Commie" to engender the intolerance of Americans? The facts, in 1954 and 1973, indicate that Americans were willing to give the benefit of the doubt to those accused of but who denied being Communists. In both surveys citizens were asked about

Table 8. Tolerance for Suspected and Admitted Communists, 1954 and 1973.

Percent of Public Who Would Allow:	1954		1973	
	Denies Being a Communist	Admitted Communist	Denies Being a Communist	Admitted Communist
Store clerk to keep job	81	25	84	57
Person to speak in community	70	27	71	53
College teacher to keep job	69	6	71	30

a man whose loyalty had been questioned before a congressional committee, but who swore under oath that he was not a Communist. Table 8 shows us how the cross section of the nation responded to this question and, for comparison, how they responded to this question about a person who admitted he was a Communist.

Although the data presented in Table 8 on *admitted* Communists are not likely to be very satisfying to civil libertarians, there is good reason to believe that Americans, in the past and more recently, are cautious about prejudging *alleged* Communists. In 1954 and in 1973 most citizens would not deny a store clerk or even a college teacher a job because a congressional committee questioned his loyalty, nor would they prohibit such a person from speaking in their community. The tactics of Senator McCarthy and contemporary McCarthylike tactics may be effective for a while, but these data strongly suggest that they run counter to the fundamental fairness of Americans. These findings, of course, are of little consolation to those injured by such tactics. Nor are they of much comfort to those who hold deviant political ideologies and expect to retain their jobs as college teachers. There continues to be a hard-core minority of the citizenry who are unwavering in their anti–civil libertarian attitudes, even toward those who are accused of but deny having Communist affiliations.

Scale of Willingness to Tolerate Nonconformists

In the preceding discussions we analyzed responses to specific questions about nonconformists. Throughout the remainder of this book, we shall rely on a scale that combines responses to fifteen questions as a basic measure of tolerance. It is convenient to use this Scale of Willingness to Tolerate Nonconformists, as Stouffer called it, but convenience is not the only or even the most important reason for using the Tolerance Scale.

A quick review of the results already presented will remind the reader that even though all the questions were intended to measure how Americans felt about nonconformists, there was considerable variation of responses from one question to the next. Some of this variation may be attributed to errors in recording or processing answers. We tried to make sure, however, that these kinds of errors were infrequent; for example, after all the questionnaires were in and the answers were carefully translated into computer codes, we made a double check on the coding and the punching of data cards.

Once one has done everything possible to minimize errors in the raw data, there are additional techniques to reduce further the effects of errors from the interview or data processing. One procedure is to scale a variety of questions. Stouffer's study dictated which questions to scale, since one of our primary purposes is to compare results in 1954 with those in 1973. Questions about Communists dominated the set used because Communists were the nonconformists foremost in people's minds in 1954. The 1954 and 1973 studies used the Guttman scale on different questions. The details of the scaling procedure used to develop the Scale of Willingness to Tolerate Nonconformists are in the Appendix. The Guttman scaling procedure required that items used have a reliable pattern. The extent to which the items do form a pattern is determined from the actual responses to the questions, not just from what one would expect to occur. An acceptable Guttman scale must achieve a pattern with minimal errors.

Minimizing errors is an important reason for relying on a scale, but scaling is also employed to extract any common content that may exist among a variety of questions. The Scale of Willingness to Tolerate Nonconformists was constructed to produce a measure that would be a more general indicator of tolerance than would be a single question about a specific subject in a narrowly defined situation. The specific nonconformists used in the 1954 and 1973 surveys were Communists (admitted and alleged), Socialists, and atheists. Situations included, among others, removing books by nonconformists from the library, allowing nonconformists to speak in the community, allowing nonconformists to teach in schools, and allowing nonconformists to work in the entertainment industry, a defense plant, or as store clerks. If tolerance for ideological nonconformity as conceived here is an attitude that extends beyond a highly specific subject and situation, then it is reasonable to expect that responses to questions about giving civil liberties to Communists, Socialists, and atheists in a variety of situations should scale in a meaningful way.

The fact that the results already presented produced a fairly consistent pattern strongly suggests that a scale could be developed that would fathom a range of common content present in the attitude called tolerance. The investigators of the 1973 survey could be even more confident than Stouffer about the scalability of the questions. We had the advantage of knowing that Stouffer, by employing exactly the same questions and procedures we used, produced a methodologically satisfactory scale. The Tolerance Scale, in 1954 and in 1973, met acceptable standards for reproducibility, minimal marginal reproducibility, and scalability.

Each respondent was placed on the Tolerance Scale using scores ranging from 0 to 5. To simplify matters, both studies combined scale scores into three categories: (1) "more tolerant," those who scored 4 or 5; (2) "less tolerant," those who scored 0 or 1; and (3) "in between," those who scored 2 or 3 on the Tolerance Scale.

We must raise a final and important question about what the scale measures. The questions that compose the scale focus almost exclusively on matters related to Communists. It is reasonable to wonder, therefore, if the scale is measuring only tolerance in the narrow sense of attitudes toward Communists. There are indications that Americans may be becoming more concerned about other types of nonconformists, such as drug pushers and purveyors of pornography. Hence, intolerance may have merely shifted from Communists to "new" nonconformists. While recognizing the salience of political climates for attitudes toward ideological nonconformists, we try to demonstrate here why the scale is a reliable measure of tolerance in a more general sense than the Communist-related scale items suggest.

The most critical question about the validity of the Tolerance Scale is how the political climate affects people's responses to political deviants. Implicit in the question is a concern about the generalizability of the scale and the impact of the level of Communist threat on political tolerance. If we are to claim that the Tolerance Scale taps a reasonably stable commitment (or lack of it) to the spirit of the Bill of Rights, we must demonstrate that the scale is generalizable and does not merely register perceived threat at the time of commitment.

At the onset of the discussion, however, we should recognize that a completely satisfactory resolution of the problem appears impossible. Intolerance by its nature is rooted in a subjective sense of danger or threat. Tolerance is possible because the tolerant person is not gripped by fear but feels that even in the face of an objective threat he or she has some comprehension of the matter and some capacity to cope with the situation. Such an interpretation would help explain why the *perceived* threat of Communism has declined when in fact the *objective* threat seems more possible in contemporary times than in the McCarthy era, as the historical review in Chapter One suggested, and as a recent study by the Brookings Institute indicated (*New York Times*, 1976b).

Furthermore, Sniderman (1975) and DiPalma and McClosky (1970) empirically demonstrated that suspicion, low self-esteem, and powerlessness, which not only make a person an instrument of fear but also seriously retard political learning, characterize those weakly committed to democratic principles. If tolerant attitudes are closely linked with personality styles as well as immediate situational demands, how is it possible to disentangle separate effects? Has tolerance increased because perceived threat has diminished? Or has perceived threat declined as a consequence of the elevation of tolerance levels in the society? Obviously a carefully controlled experimental research design would be required to even approach an understanding of the problem, but even such an experiment would be unlikely to come up with an unambiguous answer.

We have already seen that Americans in 1954 and 1973 were fair minded when there was reasonable doubt about a person's political nonconformity. However, when nonconformity was admitted, tolerance was less willingly extended. Such differences in tolerance surely suggest that threat effects are likely to be present in the Tolerance Scale. Nevertheless, threat is not the essence of what the Tolerance Scale measures. Based on a procedure described by Duncan (1969), estimates were made of what the mean level of tolerance would be if the level of perceived threat from Communists were the same in 1973 as it had been in 1954. The result was that mean tolerance was reduced only to 3.43 from 3.55 (a completely tolerant sample would have a mean of 5.00).

Data from the NORC General Social Surveys of 1972-1974 also indicate that during the time when great emphasis was given to detente with Communist countries (and by a president who was a vehement anti-Communist during the McCarthy era), the increase in tolerance for Communists was only a few percentage points greater than the increase in tolerance for Socialists or atheists. If the political mood of the country were a major source of variation in tolerance, greater change would be expected under such conditions. Political climate then would appear to affect levels of tolerance, but the claim that tolerance as measured by the Tolerance Scale is mostly a consequence of immediate climate does not seem warranted.

Central to our concern about the generalizability of the Tolerance Scale is whether or not the universalistic quality of the Bill of Rights is captured. By our definition, if one is tolerant, there are rights that will be granted within the law, even to those most condemned. To determine if the Tolerance Scale does in fact capture this spirit, two questions were used; one determined whether particular activities were *approved* of, and the second determined whether the same activities would be *allowed*. The three activities—demonstrating against a war such as the one in Vietnam; showing an X-rated movie; and teaching about sex in the schools—were not related to Communism but did involve contemporary legal issues that are closely related to civil liberties.

By combining approve-disapprove and allow-disallow responses, we derive an indicator that begins to isolate the universalistic quality which encourages citizens to extend rights to those who participate in disapproved activities. Thus, if a respondent says that he does not approve of one of the activities (or if he qualifies his answer by saying it "depends") and then says he would allow the activity anyway, he is expressing a tolerant attitude. Those who disapprove but qualify their opinion about allowing the activity may be considered somewhat less tolerant, and those who disapprove and say they would not allow the activity are the least tolerant. Approval of an activity precludes measuring whether that person will grant rights to people who behave in ways he or she disapproves of; at the least, however, we know these people are willing to extend rights to people who participate in these legal activities.

Similar response patterns for each activity were found when level of tolerance was cross tabulated with the combination indicator. Table 9 presents the data. Although it is impossible to determine whether those who both approve and allow the activities are expressing the universalistic quality we are attempting to measure, the similar distributions on the Tolerance Scale for those who disapprove-allow and approve-allow (especially in contrast to other combinations) suggest that the Tolerance Scale captures something of that spirit.

For example, those who give definite or qualified disapproval to demonstrating against a war such as the one in Vietnam and would not allow it are clearly the least likely to be "more tolerant" on the Tolerance Scale. By contrast, whereas those who definitely approve and allow such demonstrations are slightly more tolerant than those who give definite or qualified disapproval but would definitely allow it, both types are markedly more tolerant than the first two types, who express less of the spirit of the Bill of Rights. Overall, the Tolerance Scale shows substantial correlations with the combination measures presented in Table 9: .41 for demonstrating against a war like the one in Vietnam, .39 for showing X-rated movies, and .38 for teaching about sex in the schools. Thus, the Tolerance Scale does appear to be sensitive to a domain of tolerant attitudes not directly linked to Communism.

Evidence from the National Opinion Research Center's (NORC) General Social Surveys also supports our claim that the Tolerance Scale taps more than tolerance of Communists, Socialists, and atheists. The NORC surveys included some of Stouffer's questions about these three types of nonconformists as well as questions about nonconformists of the political right and homosexuals. Analyses of those data showed that people more tolerant of the political left were

Table 9. Alternative Measures of Tolerance and Tolerance Scale.

| | *Tolerance Scale Scores:* | | | |
Measure	*Percent Less Tolerant*	*Percent In-Between*	*Percent More Tolerant*	*Number*
Demonstrating against a war such as the one in Vietnam				
Definite or qualified disapproval and definitely not allow	24	40	36	1,432
Definite or qualified disapproval and allow with qualifications	13	33	54	277
Definite or qualified disapproval and definitely allow	9	21	70	447
Definitely approve and allow	5	17	78	1,170
Showing X-rated movies				
Definite or qualified disapproval and definitely not allow	23	38	39	1,898
Definite or qualified disapproval and allow with qualifications	10	24	65	203
Definite or qualified disapproval and definitely allow	5	18	77	346
Definitely approve and allow	4	15	82	924
Teaching about sex in the schools				
Definite or qualified disapproval and definitely not allow	32	43	25	695
Definite or qualified disapproval and allow with qualifications	24	36	40	276
Definite or qualified disapproval and definitely allow	16	34	50	177
Definitely approve and allow	9	23	68	2,306

also more likely to be tolerant of the political right; those tolerant of Communists were also more likely to be tolerant of homosexuals.

Finally, if the Tolerance Scale measures an underlying general tolerance, one might expect that those categorized as more tolerant by the scale would demonstrate the same kind of democratic restraint toward children that they show toward political and religious non-conformists. The 1973 study asked about child-rearing attitudes that convey a person's response to nonconformity in children. The state-ments to which respondents could agree or disagree were: (1) if a child is unusual in any way, his parents should get him to be more like other children; and (2) a child should never be allowed to talk back to his parents because he will then lose respect for them. Replies to both statements were correlated with the Tolerance Scale scores (.33 for the first and .36 for the second statement). Such correlations, although not conventionally considered large, supported assump-tions of generalizability of the Tolerance Scale.

Still another concern about the validity of the Tolerance Scale is the question of respondent indifference. Are those who are more tolerant on the Tolerance Scale merely expressing indifference to other people, conformists or nonconformists? The data tell us that tolerance is not just apathy. Consistently, across time and within each survey, the more tolerant are substantially the most active, most inter-ested, and best educated, as Chapter Ten demonstrates in detail. In short, the more tolerant appear to be the opposite of indifferent, so there is no reason to believe those who score highest on the Tolerance Scale do so out of indifference or apathy.

We believe that all the evidence we have presented indicates that the Tolerance Scale continues to perform well and adequately taps levels of commitment to the fundamental principles of the Bill of Rights. Indeed, Stouffer appears to have been overly cautious in his interpretation of what the scale measures. But regardless of the scale's virtues, both studies included a variety of civil liberties questions hav-ing no direct bearing on Communists, and these items will be utilized to supplement our findings from the Tolerance Scale.*

*Presser and Schuman (1975) performed a series of experiments on question wording that demonstrate the importance of not relying on single indicators—a single item or scale. They also noted that the Stouffer tolerance questions made libertarian responses more difficult than a slightly varied

Changes in Tolerance: 1954–1973

Have Americans changed in their commitment to civil liberties? As a first step in this assessment, we look at how rank-and-file citizens and their community leaders have altered their willingness to extend civil liberties to people whose ideas and practices differ from the mainstream. The results from the Tolerance Scale tell us that the changes have been substantial (Table 10). Americans and their local

**Table 10. Willingness to Tolerate Nonconformists,
for Community Leaders and National Cross Section, 1954 and 1973.**

	Tolerance Scale Scores:			
Sample	*Percent Less Tolerant*	*Percent In-Between*	*Percent More Tolerant*	*Number*
1954				
Community leaders	5	29	66	1,500
National cross section	19	50	31	4,933
1973				
Community leaders	4	13	83	649
National cross section	16	25	55	3,539

leaders were more willing in 1973 than in 1954 to grant nonconformists their constitutionally prescribed liberties. Perhaps the most significant change has been that a majority of Americans can now be called more tolerant. This is a critical shift since the existence of a tolerant majority greatly enhances the prospect that expansion of support for civil liberties will be accelerated.

Community leaders continue to have a higher proportion of more tolerant people than the nationwide sample, but both have

---

form of the same question. However, since education is more highly correlated with the Stouffer question format than the alternative ("easier") form, changes over time in the Stouffer question responses may be partly an artifact of expanding sophistication (education). Since we find tolerance has increased in all educational categories, our basic conclusions would still hold. Furthermore, we also argue that sophistication itself is intimately linked to tolerance; hence, referring to results as artifacts is somewhat misleading.

shown sizable gains: only 66 percent of the leaders and 31 percent of the cross-sectional sample in 1954 scored as more tolerant; by 1973, 83 percent of the leaders and 55 percent of the rank and file were more tolerant.

There are several observations to be made about these results. First, in 1954 the plurality of leaders were more tolerant, and the plurality of the cross section were in between; by 1973 the plurality of both the leaders and the general public were more tolerant. Second, the percentage gap between leaders and the rank and file is closing, so that the 1973 cross section is looking more like local leaders in its distribution of scale scores than it did in 1954. Finally, the small but hard-core minority of less tolerant types in both samples in the 1954 and 1973 surveys should be noted. Exactly who these less tolerant Americans are, and why they are, will become clearer as we consider these questions in more detailed analyses.

When we look at specific local leaders (Table 11), we find, as we did earlier, that each type of leader (except for American Legion commanders in 1973) was more tolerant than the national cross section. Moreover, all leader categories, with the exception of local labor union leaders, registered a gain between 1954 and 1973 in the percentage more tolerant.

Tolerance changes have not only been substantial for leaders and the national cross section, they have also been broadly based. The details of how pervasive the gains have been will be discussed in succeeding chapters of this book. Shifts toward greater tolerance have occurred in every major demographic category—men and women, old and young, southerners and nonsoutherners, educated and uneducated. For many people, these findings may seem solid and even reassuring, but much more ground must be covered to get a firmer fix on these changes, not the least of which is attention to other measures of democratic restraint.

So far we have been concerned with the Tolerance Scale as a measure of changes in support for civil liberties, but the trend of greater respect for the civil liberties of others is also evident in differently worded questions. The shift between 1954 and 1973 was not always as substantial as that indicated by the Tolerance Scale, but Americans are changing in their unwillingness to permit the govern-

Table 11. Percent More Tolerant on the Tolerance Scale, by Type of Leader, 1954 and 1973.

Type of Leader	Percent More Tolerant:	
	1954	1973
Public officials		
Mayors	60	90
Presidents, school board	62	92
Presidents, library board	79	96
Police chiefs	—	77
Political party chairmen		
Republican county central committee	70	85
Democratic county central committee	64	79
Industrial leaders		
Presidents, Chamber of Commerce	65	84
Presidents, labor union	62	58
Heads of special patriotic groups		
Commanders, American Legion	46	55
Regents, DAR	48	—
Others		
Chairmen, Community Chest	82	86
Presidents, bar association	77	92
Newspaper publishers	84	85
Presidents, women's club	49	—
Presidents, League of Women Voters	—	94
Presidents, Parent-Teacher Associations	68	84
All community leaders	66	83
National cross section	31	55

ment to wiretap Communists' phones (from 27 to 49 percent), in their willingness to protect the rights of innocent people even if some Communists are not discovered (from 32 to 70 percent), and in their judgment that it is a bad idea to report a suspected Communist to the FBI (from 20 to 31 percent). Although libertarian responses were not given by a majority of the public, as was true when using the Tolerance Scale, in two out of the three items the antilibertarians also failed to achieve a majority.

Changes in Tolerance: 1972-1977

Are the changes in tolerance reported for the 1954–1973 period continuing? One might assume that revelations of violations of civil liberties by the Nixon administration would have greatly sensitized Americans to such issues and would have encouraged a greater appreciation of democratic restraint. Recent evidence indicates that something between the spring of 1973 and the spring of 1974, most likely the Watergate scandals, had an astonishing impact on Americans' attitudes toward government wiretapping, but tolerance showed little change. All but the 1973 wiretapping data presented in Table 12

Table 12. Attitude Toward Government Wiretapping, 1973–1977.

Attitude	Percent in 1973[a]	Percent in 1974	Percent in 1975	Percent in 1977
Approve	52	16	16	19
Disapprove	44	80	80	78
No opinion	4	4	4	3

[a] Percent represents the average responses to four questions about wiretapping Communists, college demonstrators, drug pushers, and organized criminals. The 1974 and 1975 NORC question reads: *"Everything considered, would you say that in general you approve or disapprove of wiretapping?"*

came from the NORC General Social Surveys (sample size generally around 1,500); the 1973 wiretapping data are from our tolerance survey. The findings in Table 12 for the 1973–1974 time period are extraordinary if adjustment of the 1973 data is reasonable. However, even allowing for differences in question wording, we should still find a sizable shift. In 1973, 44 percent disapproved of government wiretapping. By 1974, 80 percent disapproved, and about the same proportion continues to disapprove.

Recent changes in tolerance for atheists and Socialists have been slight, but tolerance for Communists and homosexuals has shifted more markedly, and in a direction consistent with the trends from 1954 to 1973 (Table 13). Willingness to extend civil liberties to Communists, however, appears to have leveled off from 1973–1974 levels, when detente with Communist countries was most likely to

Table 13. Tolerance for Communists, Atheists, Socialists, and Homosexuals, 1972–1977.

Type of Nonconformist	Percent Tolerant in:				
	1972	1973	1974	1976	1977
Communist					
College teacher	32	39	42	41	39
Books in library	53	58	59	56	55
Speaker in community	52	60	58	55	55
Atheist					
College teacher	40	41	42	41	39
Books in library	61	61	60	60	59
Speaker in community	65	65	62	64	62
Socialist					
College teacher	56	58	57	—	—
Books in library	68	71	69	—	—
Speaker in community	77	77	76	—	—
Homosexual					
College teacher	—	61	62	52	49
Books in library	—	47	50	55	55
Speaker in community	—	54	55	62	62

Source: General Social Surveys, National Opinion Research Center, University of Chicago.

have affected these attitudes. The most surprising exception to the overall trends is the precipitous drop in academic freedom extended to homosexuals. Whereas tolerance for homosexuals has clearly increased in other areas, there has been a 12 percent drop in tolerance for homosexual professors between 1974 and 1977.

The comparison of tolerance for Communists and homosexuals is of particular interest here in view of concerns about how broadly tolerance extends. Except for freedom of the press, which is comparable for Communists and homosexuals, academic freedom and freedom of speech are more willingly extended for homosexuals than for Communists. In 1977, 39 percent of the national sample would allow a Communist to teach in a college or university. A majority of Americans in 1976, 52 percent, granted academic freedom to homosexuals, but this figure slipped to 49 percent in 1977. Freedom of the press for both was comparable in 1977, but allowing a homosexual to speak in the community was more tolerable (62 percent) than allowing a Communist to have his say (55 percent). The reasonably similar responses to Communists and homosexuals, as well as to atheists, suggest that American tolerance, as measured here, is not narrowly confined.

Summary of Findings

By 1973 a majority of Americans scored as more tolerant (55 percent) on the Tolerance Scale, a substantial gain over the meager 31 percent in 1954. The change has been broadly based, but leaders continue to be more tolerant than rank-and-file citizens. Furthermore, the increase in tolerance continued into 1976, but tolerance of some nonconformists appeared to be leveling off and in several instances ran counter to previous trends.

We also found that when forced to choose between hurting some innocent people to discover all the Communists or protecting the rights of the innocent even if some Communists are not discovered, less than a fourth chose the former alternative in 1973. Americans for the most part have been, and continue to be, fairminded; they give the accused the benefit of the doubt. Government violations of citizens' rights to privacy by wiretapping are made without the approval of most Americans. Watergate appears to have dramatically expanded public disapproval of such government invasions.

Yet all is not well with American commitment to civil liberties. The proportion of the public that was less tolerant in 1954 has since declined very little. And, although Americans have a strong commitment to fair-mindedness toward the accused who deny their nonconformity, extension of civil liberties to an admitted Communist is in some situations far less likely (for example, allowing a Communist to keep a job as a college teacher). There are still pockets of the population who appear to be outside the mainstream commitment to civil liberties, a point that will be pursued in detail in the remainder of the book.

Chapter 4

Education and Political Tolerance

/\·/\·\·/\·/\·/\·\·/\·/\·/\·\·/\·/\·/\·\·/\·/\·\·/\·/\·/\·\·/\·/\·/\·\·/\·/\·\·/\·/\·/\·\·/\·/\·\

Research in the two decades since Stouffer published *Communism, Conformity, and Civil Liberties* has greatly enriched our understanding of both the determinants and the correlates of tolerance. Throughout the period, scholars have affirmed the idea that tolerance itself is multifaceted rather than unitary. That is, even though political intolerance, ethnic prejudice, religious bigotry, racism, and other forms of intolerance are frequently found to be highly correlated with one another, they are evidently not necessarily so related.*
Often one finds one form of intolerance at high levels among a popu-

---

*The literature on tolerance broadly conceived is massive. We may cite as representative of our point here, however, one interpretative essay (Pettigrew, 1966) that focused sharply on the similarities and differences between anti-Semitism and anti-Negro attitudes; after having reviewed many studies, this source concluded: "The inference is clear: anti-Semitism and anti-Negro attitudes are by no means shaped by identical social forces; hence, they do not necessarily rise and diminish together. . . . Available evidence suggests that a reduction in prejudice against one minority *does not* necessarily lead to any increase in prejudice against another. On the contrary, prejudices against different groups, even when shaped by somewhat different social forces, are likely to decline together" (Pettigrew, 1966, pp. 392–394).

lation while other varieties are not found, and often one finds within the minds of particular individuals a high level of anti-Semitism, say, but a low level of political intolerance. Tolerance, then, is a complex phenomenon; research has shown that each variety of tolerance is a product of diverse factors as well. Thus, although the Tolerance Scale is used extensively in what follows, we try to avoid the pitfall of proceeding as though such a complex phenomenon as political tolerance could be reduced appropriately to a single measure.

The present study of political tolerance and intolerance may be viewed as centering on what Lipset and Raab (1970, p. 433) have termed "democratic restraint." Many writers have discussed the broad societal conditions that encourage democratic restraint to flourish or compel it to subside. In the society at large, transportation and communication, twin marvels of modern industrial technique, are frequently cited. Given democratic norms and institutions permitting and encouraging the free flow of persons and ideas, the elaborate modern networks of transportation and communication inspire among persons of different social strata and geographical regions a "heightened mutual awareness" that "has enlarged the internal population which dwells in the minds of men" (Shils, 1962, p. 43). Similarly, the commingling of dense populations of heterogeneous people in cities has been linked frequently to rising levels of political tolerance; this matter is examined extensively in Chapter Six. But by far the most important factor in the view of everyone who has addressed the issue of democratic restraint and political intolerance is the formal educational level of the population. Reviewing the evidence in 1959, Lipset wrote: "Data gathered by public opinion research agencies which have questioned people in different countries with regard to their belief in various democratic norms of tolerance for opposition, to their attitudes toward ethnic or racial minorities, and with regard to their belief in multiparty as against one-party systems have found that *the most important single factor differentiating those giving democratic responses from others has been education.* The higher one's education, the more likely one is to believe in democratic values and support democratic practices. All the relevant studies indicate that education is far more significant than income or occupation" (Lipset, 1959, p. 79). This assessment continues to describe research evidence accurately in 1977. For this reason the present chapter examines educational level and democratic restraint in detail, reserving for later chapters discussion of other major factors.

We should note here, however, that although we do not ignore the findings of other studies on the importance of education and of other variables, no overarching "theory" has directed this research. What Stouffer sought to do in the 1954 study was to test ideas about the well-being and viability of our democracy against empirical evidence gathered from its citizens. Although he tested many theoretical hypotheses, his interest was not to establish the tenability of any particular theory but to find out what factors strengthened or weakened civil liberties in America. In repeating Stouffer's study in 1973, we also have attempted to discover anything and everything that might be useful or harmful to the purposes of a democratic society. Thus, although we test numerous hypotheses from social scientific theories in the following pages, our purpose remains always that of Stouffer: to establish useful knowledge regarding democratic restraint and political intolerance.

Education and Tolerance Scale Scores: 1954 and 1973

Let us begin by examining the relation of education level to political tolerance as measured by Stouffer's Tolerance Scale among the two cross sections of the American public studied in 1954 and 1973; Table 14 presents the results. Table 14 contains a wealth of information, but the following points are crucial:

1. The higher the education, the higher the Tolerance Scale score, both in 1954 and in 1973. A comparison of the highest and lowest educational levels illustrates the power of this relationship: in 1954, 65 percent of the college graduates were in the more tolerant category, compared to only 14 percent of those with grade school education; in 1973, 84 percent of the college graduates were in the more tolerant category, compared to only 19 percent of those with grade school education.

2. The relationship between level of education and Tolerance Scale score was perfectly incremental, both in 1954 and in 1973. Thus, each step up the educational ladder was accompanied by a noticeable gain in the proportion scoring high on the Tolerance Scale. These stepwise increases in expressions of democratic restraint as educa-

**Table 14. Education and Political Tolerance, National Cross Section,
1954 and 1973.**

| | Tolerance Scale Scores: | | | |
Level of Education	Percent Less Tolerant	Percent In-Between	Percent More Tolerant	Number
1954				
College graduates	5	30	65	376
Some college	10	38	53	460
High school graduates	14	46	40	1,208
Some high school	19	54	27	1,022
Grade school	30	56	14	1,842
				4,908
1973				
College graduates	3	12	84	559
Some college	7	19	75	619
High school graduates	12	30	58	1,099
Some high school	20	40	40	624
Grade school	37	44	19	598
				3,499

tional level goes up suggest that schooling adds systematically to the
propensity toward political tolerance.

3. In each educational level except the lowest one, the proportion falling into the more tolerant category increased markedly
between 1954 and 1973. Even those with grade school educations in
1973 showed a higher proportion more tolerant than did their counterparts in 1954, although the increase of five percentage points was
not large. What might account for this strengthening of the relationship between education and political tolerance at each level of schooling? Why should a given level of education in 1973 seem to result in
much greater support for civil liberties than did the same amount of
schooling in 1954?

One way to discover what it is about level of education that
affects democratic restraint is to try to find out what aspects of education *do not* have such effects. If we consider, for this purpose, the different ways in which education may be construed, two relatively distinct conceptions come to mind. On the one hand, level of education
is quite commonly taken as an indicator of social position, leaving its
other potential meanings unstressed; this is the usual procedure in

social research. On the other hand, level of education may be taken as an indicator of cognitive development and cultural sophistication, in which case no essential connection between education and social position is implied.

Clearly it is as an indicator of cognitive differentiation and cultural sophistication, rather than as a mere marker of social position, that educational level can be expected to affect political tolerance. There are at least three reasons for this choice. First, the greater the schooling, the greater the likelihood of gaining specific knowledge about civil liberties and the democratic process. A second reason, more subtle but advanced by Borhek (1965, p. 91) as more important, is that with increased education comes increased awareness of the varieties of human experience that legitimize wide variation in beliefs, values, and behavior. Finally, and most important in our view, the greater the schooling, the more likely that one's cognitive development will be characterized by the flexible, rational strategies of thinking which encourage democratic restraint. Evidence supporting these assertions is presented below. For the moment, many readers probably will agree that as schooling increases, the capacity to understand the classic statement by Lippmann also rises: "And so, if we truly wish to understand why freedom is necessary in a civilized society, we must begin by realizing that, because freedom of discussion improves our own opinions, the liberties of other men are our own vital necessity" (1951, p. 401).

We can begin to distinguish the effects of the two different conceptions of educational attainment by examining the data presented in Table 15 for occupational level, a separate variable commonly accepted as a marker of social position. If educational effects on political tolerance arise mostly from experiences and influences associated with status position, then the relationship between educational level and political tolerance should diminish when results by educational level are observed within occupational status groupings. There are sizable associations between occupational status and political tolerance in both 1954 and 1973, but when educational level is conjoined with occupational level, the association between occupational status and political tolerance virtually collapses, while that between education and tolerance remains strong. Differences in tolerance scores covering persons in the same occupation grouping and different education

Table 15. Occupation, Education, and Political Tolerance,
National Cross Section, 1954 and 1973.

Level of Education	Percent Less Tolerant	Percent In-Between	Percent More Tolerant	Number
	Tolerance Scale Scores:			
White collar[a]				
Less than high school	18	52	30	335
High school	11	43	46	353
Some college	8	33	59	180
College graduate	4	27	69	235
				1,103
Blue collar[a]				
Less than high school	23	57	20	968
High school	12	50	39	261
Some college	12	35	54	69
College graduate	8	23	69	13
				1,311
White collar[b]				
Less than high school	13	47	40	143
High school	12	29	59	356
Some college	6	19	75	280
College graduate	3	12	85	431
				1,210
Blue collar[b]				
Less than high school	25	43	32	566
High school	12	30	58	343
Some college	7	19	74	117
College graduate	10	11	79	19
				1,045

[a]Refers to present occupation of respondent only; persons retired or unemployed at time of interview, persons with farm occupations, and housewives are omitted.
[b]Refers to present occupation or most recent occupation for persons retired or unemployed at time of interview; persons with farm occupations and housewives omitted.

categories are far larger—an average of 45 percentage points—than the differences in tolerance scores among persons in the same education category and different occupation groupings, which average less than 10 percentage points. In each occupation grouping, persons with different levels of schooling have quite different Tolerance Scale scores. Stated another way, in both 1954 and 1973, persons with similar education have similar Tolerance scores, irrespective of their occupational status.

The results in Table 15 establish beyond question that political tolerance is strongly affected by educational level *in its own right,* independent of any effects associated with occupational status.* Thus, some tendency to political tolerance may go along with the power and control over one's environment afforded by high occupational position, but formal schooling is the more potent source of democratic restraint. Hyman, Wright, and Reed (1975) demonstrated with data from a variety of national samples that persons with more education have more knowledge about more subjects than do persons with less education. This effect also occurs in our national sample; as shown in Table 16, persons with more schooling know much more about Communist and Nazi beliefs than do persons with less schooling. We believe, then, that level of education is strongly associated with political tolerance largely because of the greater cognitive development and cultural sophistication which accompanies increases in formal education. Our conclusion is reminiscent of that reached by Trow (1958, p. 273), who found "that political tolerance is a norm or cluster of norms, very strongly related to cultural sophistication, or 'cosmopolitanism,' and thus to the level of education achieved—*and to very little else.*"

This view of the meaning of education for political tolerance helps make sense of the dramatic rise in the expression of democratic restraint among Americans between 1954 and 1973, for it was during this period that the American people experienced a massive elevation in educational levels. In 1950, the median school years completed were 9.3; 67.5 percent of the adult population had not completed high school, and only 6.2 percent were college graduates. By 1973, the median school years completed had surged forward to 12.7; only 19.8

*Entirely comparable results with respect to relationships between occupation, education, and anti-Semitism were reported for a 1964 national sample (Selznick and Steinberg, 1969). On the other hand, Stember (1961) sharply disputed the notion that higher education is strongly associated with less anti-Semitism. In response to Stember's position, Schwartz (1967) reviewed her assessment of national sample data on anti-Negro attitudes and concluded: "Our own conclusions remain that, for the issue considered here, there is a clear-cut association between education and attitudes toward integration" (Schwartz, 1967, p. 120).

Table 16. Level of Education and Knowledge of
Communism and Nazism, 1973.

Level of Education	Percent Having No Knowledge	Percent Knowing One Belief	Percent Knowing Two or More Beliefs	Number
Knowledge of Communism				
Less than high school	52	25	23	1,222
High school	29	33	38	1,099
Some college	23	33	44	619
College graduate	20	36	44	559
				3,499
Knowledge of Nazism				
Less than high school	75	18	7	1,222
High school	59	27	14	1,099
Some college	47	32	21	619
College graduate	29	38	33	559
				3,499

percent had completed less than high school, while 19.0 percent had attained four years of college or more (U.S. Bureau of the Census, 1974, Table 186, p. 116).

An examination of changes in perceptions of Communist threat affords another revealing perspective on the nature of the relationship between education and tolerance. Stouffer (1955) predicted that a decline in the perception of Communist threat would be accompanied by a rise in tolerance for nonconformists. In 1954, nearly half (43 percent) of the national sample respondents perceived American Communists as posing a "very great" or "great" danger, whereas in 1973 only 28 percent of the respondents perceived Communists as posing such a serious threat. Along with this change in political climate over the two time periods studied, there is a change in the relation of education to perception of Communist danger. In 1954, when the perception of danger from American Communists had a firmer purchase on reality than in 1973, there was not much difference in educational level among persons classified as high in perceptions of Communist threat–high in Tolerance Scale score, as middle threat–high tolerance, and as low threat–high tolerance. But in 1973, when any evidence of threat from internal Communism was far more difficult to come by than in 1954, the educational level of the low threat–high tolerance group is much higher (62 percent with some college training or more) than that among the middle threat–high tolerance group (47 percent with any college training), which, in turn, is notably higher than that among the high threat–high tolerance group (only 31 percent with any college training).

These strikingly different patterns of association between educational level, perception of Communist danger, and Tolerance Scale score, occurring under the different political climates of 1954 and 1973, provide further support for the view that educational attainment affects tolerance primarily because the more educated are more cognitively able and more culturally sophisticated. Thus, when some (although not much) objective evidence of an internal danger from Communist sources exists, as it did in 1954, the better-educated persons should be distributed across the perception of Communist threat response categories rather evenly, and they are. And when virtually no evidence of internal danger from Communism is present, as in 1973, then the better-educated people should pile up in the low threat–high tolerance response category, and they do.

It is possible, of course, to attribute too much civilizing power to formal schooling. The point can be illustrated well by focusing on the persons scoring high on the Tolerance Scale, a much more highly educated group than other sets of respondents. Even these highly educated persons, both in 1954 and in 1973, show considerable willingness to endorse such intolerant practices as tapping telephones to get evidence on suspected Communists or reporting suspected Communists to the FBI. These propensities were greater in 1954 than in 1973, reflecting the different political climates of the two periods, but even in 1973 more than half of the persons scoring high on the Tolerance Scale and perceiving great Communist danger endorse the wiretapping and FBI-alerting options. The sense of these data seems to be that increases in educational level may not be expected to produce comparable gains in political tolerance with respect to specific agents (in this case, suspected Communists) among persons who continue to view the agents as potential threats to the nation. Thus, although it is probably true that levels of political tolerance will be higher, *other things equal,* when average levels of education among the population increase, increments in educational level *alone* do not automatically bring about greater political tolerance. It is essential, for example, to consider the political climates prevailing at specific times, since these will always contribute in some measure to the extent of democratic restraint among the population.

This point is not novel; it was stressed by Glazer and Lipset (1955) in their review of Stouffer's 1954 study. After having observed that political tolerance was greater in the United States during the 1930s and World War II than it was in the 1950s, they concluded (pp. 151–152): "Obviously, the increase in intolerance is not a result of the fact that there now are more poorly educated people, or that the farm population has increased. The reverse is, of course, true. The important factor which has affected the degree of tolerance is the political problem of Communism and how to deal with it, which is intimately related to the state of civil liberties. But this question is more dependent on changes in international affairs and domestic American politics than on the raising of the educational level." The authors went on to relate that a change in the policy of the leaders of the Republican party toward Senator McCarthy "sharply changed the climate of opinion within a short space of time" (p. 153), illustrating further the importance of the political situation in altering levels of tolerance. A comparative study of political tolerance in England and the United States in the 1950s also made this point forcefully (Hyman, 1963, p. 245): "In summary, it appeared that official security procedures in England had been applied to a much smaller number of individuals within a relatively narrow sector of the society. The law of parsimony would suggest that the differences in the climate of political intolerance and the corollary atmosphere of fear in the fifties in the United States and England were a simple function of the magnitude of official investigation rather than a product of complex social, historical, and psychological variables."

Although we need not go so far as Hyman in attributing changes in political tolerance exclusively to contemporaneous factors in the political situation, our present evidence agrees with him and with Glazer and Lipset in finding the political climate an important factor in determining levels of democratic restraint. A twofold conclusion seems prudent: at a given level of perceived threat, a more highly educated population will be more politically tolerant than a less-educated population; at the same time, increases in the educational level of a population will not produce sharp increases in political tolerance if the perception of internal danger (as, for example, from Communism) among the population is widespread.

Distinguishing the Politically Tolerant in 1973

The contribution made by education to the expression of political tolerance in the United States today can be better understood by reviewing additional information elicited in the 1973 study. For example, persons in 1973 who perceived little danger from internal Communism and scored high on Stouffer's Tolerance Scale—by far the most highly educated group, it will be recalled—are clearly the most steadfast in supporting traditional civil liberties. In addition to the question about listening in on telephone conversations of suspected Communists, asked in both studies, the 1973 study asked the same question about college demonstrators, drug pushers, and members of organized crime. As disclosed by the data in Table 17, a major-

Table 17. Perception of Communist Threat, Tolerance Scale Score, and Disposition to Oppose Listening In on Conversations of College Demonstrators, Drug Pushers, and Members of Organized Crime, 1973.

Perception of Communist Threat	Tolerance Scale Score	Percent Answering:			
		Should Listen	Should Not Listen	No Opinion	Number
College demonstrators					
Low	High	11	87	2	711
Middle	High	22	76	2	686
High	High	28	69	3	384
Drug pushers					
Low	High	51	48	1	707
Middle	High	64	34	2	688
High	High	69	29	2	384
Members of organized crime					
Low	High	54	45	1	710
Middle	High	65	33	2	688
High	High	69	28	3	384

ity in all three of the high tolerance groups endorsed bugging the telephones of drug pushers and organized crime members. Nevertheless, the low threat–high tolerance respondents are considerably more protective of the civil rights of such persons, as well as of the much more benignly viewed college demonstrators, than are persons in either of the other two groups.

Even in the case of a question deliberately worded to evoke stress among those providing an intolerant response, the greater political tolerance of the low threat–high tolerance group is maintained. We asked: *"In your opinion, which of these two is more important? 1. To find out all the Communists even if some innocent people should be hurt; 2. To protect the rights of innocent people, even if some Communists are not found out."* Responses endorsing the "protect innocent people" alternative varied from a high of 92 percent among persons in the low threat–high tolerance group to a low of 43 percent among persons in the high threat–low tolerance group.

Of those scoring high on the Tolerance Scale, persons in the low threat–high tolerance group are considerably more highly educated than are persons in the middle threat–high tolerance group or in the high threat–high tolerance group. On a variety of questions dealing with civil liberties, the high tolerance groups consistently have much higher proportions giving tolerant responses than do other groups; and of these groups, the low threat–high tolerance group *always leads by large margins* in supporting the politically tolerant position. These additional 1973 data, set alongside the 1954 and 1973 results already discussed, provide mounting evidence that educational attainment is associated both with realistic estimates of internal danger and with enlightened attitudes supporting traditional American civil liberties.

The picture of the politically tolerant persons in 1973 can be sharpened by examining information in two further areas: the domain of political interests, identification, and involvement; and the sphere of religious beliefs and commitments. We sought to gauge the sense of social and political competence among respondents by the following two questions: (1) *"Has a friend or acquaintance recently asked your opinion about social or political issues?"* and (2) *"Compared to others belonging to your circle of friends, are you more or less likely to be asked for your opinions on social and political issues?"* The answers to these two questions exhibit two trends: (1) persons in the three high tolerance groups emerge as more socially and politically competent in their own estimations than do members of the other groups; and (2) persons in the low threat–high tolerance group stand out from all others as being most secure in their sense of social and political competence. Patterns comparable to these are also present for the low threat–high tolerance group, which shows a higher degree of interest in national politics, greater party identification as an "Independent" rather than as a Democrat or Republican, and more likelihood to have voted in the 1972 Presidential election than do other groups.

We measured religious beliefs and commitments through an index of religious orthodoxy developed from a set of four questions concerning the existence and nature of God, the Devil, Jesus Christ, and Biblical miracles. The index ranges from a position of having very little of the traditional sorts of beliefs in these agents and events to a position of having very strong, traditional beliefs in them. Perhaps by now the reader will not be surprised to observe, in Table 18, that the low threat–high tolerance group differs from other groups on this index; yet the extent of the dissimilarity in response of this group from all the others is startling. The low threat–high tolerance group has a much lower proportion of religiously orthodox persons than do

Table 18. Perception of Communist Threat, Tolerance Scale Score, and Degree of Religious Orthodoxy, 1973.

Perception of Communist Threat	Tolerance Scale Score	Degree of Religious Orthodoxy:			
		Percent Low	Percent Middle	Percent High	Number
Low	High	44	28	28	713
Middle	High	23	28	49	688
Low	Middle	16	29	55	139
High	High	14	23	63	385
Middle	Middle	12	22	66	329
Low	Low	9	23	68	56
High	Middle	6	14	80	404
High	Low	4	18	78	233
Middle	Low	3	17	80	144
Not classifiable		17	19	64	455

all the remaining groups. Only the 1973 data on the disposition to report suspected Communists to the FBI show a discrepancy between the low threat–high tolerance group and the rest of the groups as sharp as appears here in the case of religious orthodoxy. Thus, in seeking to distinguish the politically tolerant persons in 1973, we may now add relatively great freedom from conventional religious dogma and tradition to their characteristics. Such freedom from orthodox religious views bespeaks, again, the cultivated mind we have been describing as the product of high educational attainment, which in turn sustains the highest levels of commitment to democratic restraint.

The Problem of Response-Set

Interpreting attitudinal differences among persons with varying amounts of education when the attitude measure is a straightforward statement or question with an agree-disagree or approve-disapprove form of response is plagued by the problem of acquiescent response-set. The difficulty arises from the readiness of less-educated persons, operating presumably from a cognitively restricted, unsophisticated frame of reference, to seize on the positive alternatives presented to them, often while ignoring the content of the question. The better-educated, meanwhile, exercising the greater discrimination with which their schooling has equipped them, attend more to the content of the item and do not accumulate unthinkingly in categories of positive response. This process may result in distributions showing strong relationships between education and the attitudes measured, if the meanings of the items presented the respondent all flow in one direction. It is then ambiguous whether the link between educational level and attitude marks a genuine difference in attitude between educational groups or is instead a difference artificially forged by the biased response tendencies of the less-educated.

The present study is vexed with this problem as a consequence of decisions taken self-consciously in repeating Stouffer's 1954 study. We chose to try to maximize comparability with the earlier work by retaining most of its measures. Although some new questions were asked in 1973, we kept Stouffer's basic questions measuring political tolerance, and some of these questions might produce response bias.

Fortunately, there are ways of reducing the ambiguity that the possibility of acquiescent response-set brings to the education-tolerance relationship. It may be suggested in the first place that the propensity toward acquiescent response bias on the part of the less-educated may be less pronounced than some researchers have thought. We have seen, for example, that scores on the Tolerance Scale increased from 1954 to 1973 at every educational level. Since the acquiescent response-set should lead to *low* tolerance scores among the less-educated, proponents of the theory that response-set explains the relationship between educational level and tolerance are faced with accounting for these increases within educational levels.

More important, perhaps, are the many systematic relationships reviewed in this chapter between perception of Communist threat, Tolerance Scale score, and other variables. According to the theory of response bias, the less-educated should be heavily overrepresented among those who perceive the Communist threat to be great, but no such regularity appears in the data. Indeed, the results presented for the Communist threat–Tolerance Scale analytic groups present numerous relationships that are readily understandable in terms of genuine differences between educational groups but that pose severe problems for the response-bias theory to resolve.

Another empirical approach to reducing ambiguity of interpretation of attitudinal differences between educational groupings was that worked out by Jackman (1973), who developed path analytic models for testing the response-bias theory against other theories in explaining relationships between educational level and anti-Semitism. Unfortunately, this procedure requires both an attitude measure that is subject to response bias and a measure *not* open to response bias, a condition not met by our data. For the reasons noted above, however, an acquiescent response-set interpretation of differences in political tolerance between educational groups seems difficult to maintain for the data of the present study.

The Problem of Educational Selection

Our view that political tolerance is in large part a consequence of the knowledge, cognitive skills, and cultural sophistication which are acquired normally through advanced schooling is also challenged by the theory of educational selection. The central idea of the educational selection theory is that the schools are basically processing plants, which at various times cull out students lacking the qualities thought necessary to pursue lines of study leading to some higher level of educational training while selecting into the more advanced tracks of study the students possessing the prized qualities. The sorting and selecting process occurs partly through the channeling of students into different courses of study that omit or provide the prerequisites for subsequent work. In high school, for example, students may be channeled into vocational, business, or college preparatory tracks; in college, undergraduate students may be offered either the "general" courses or the "preprofessional" courses, and some graduate students are steered toward the "terminal" master's degree, while others are directed on to the doctorate. Part of the selection process also takes place at entry, so that, as Feldman and Newcomb (1969, p. 144) noted regarding college matriculation, "the more prestigious the institution, the more likely it is to attract and to admit those students who have already most nearly attained the characteristics of an 'educated man.'"

The educational selection theory can be best conveyed by briefly reviewing some research on schooling and equality. A number of scholars in recent years have demonstrated that increasing education does not materially reduce inequality. In particular, Boudon (1974) established beyond question that a society's stratification system holds the key to inequality, not its educational system. With regard to educational growth specifically, he reported (p. 187) that "other things equal, and under broad conditions, educational growth as such has the effect of increasing rather than decreasing social and economic inequality, even in the case of an educational system that becomes more equalitarian."

Although Boudon did not speculate on the implications of his work for any attitudinal consequences of educational growth, Jencks and his associates did make such consequences explicit: "In the absence of evidence, we are inclined to believe that the relationship between schooling and noncognitive traits is much like the relationship between schooling and cognitive traits. We believe, in other words, that noncognitive differences between the highly educated and the poorly educated derive primarily from selection. But we also assume that staying in school has a modest effect on many of the non-cognitive traits that employers value" (Jencks and others, 1972, p. 134). Based on the Jencks interpretation, the increased political tolerance of the American people over the past two decades—which we have been attributing largely to greater cognitive skills and cultural sophistication acquired through increased amounts of schooling—is best considered a consequence of the process of selecting the already-tolerant persons to receive the greater amounts of schooling. In this view, the origins of tolerance should be sought among the factors producing educational selection rather than within the process of education itself.

Analyzing factors important in educational selection, Feldman and Newcomb cite level of intelligence and socioeconomic status as "two of the most important determinants"; they add "size and type of community of residence, size of high school, size of family, and race and religion" as other selection variables affecting college enrollment (Feldman and Newcomb, 1969, pp. 106–108). In this book we consider all these variables except intelligence and size of high school, for which we have no data (Williams, Nunn, and St. Peter, 1976a and 1976b). In all the analyses we have carried out, we have found no evidence that educational selection is more fundamental in producing political tolerance than is educational level as such; rather, our analyses reveal the paramount importance of educational level in affecting levels of political tolerance. Williams, Nunn, and St. Peter also reported that educational level retains much the strongest association with political tolerance when effects on tolerance of education, city size, region, exposure to mass media news, gender, and occupation are assessed simultaneously.

However, we must note that no satisfactory test between the educational selection theory and our stress on educational process in affecting democratic restraint is possible with present data. Such a test would require measures of tolerance for the same persons at different times in their lives, both during and after they had completed their schooling; only with such information can the differential effects of the selection process and the educational process be untangled definitively.

Some good evidence exists, however, on the impact of both educational selection and educational process. Feldman and

Newcomb, reviewing differences between college freshmen and college seniors from different studies, found that: "Nearly without
exception, the studies show seniors to be less authoritarian, less dogmatic, less ethnocentric, and less prejudiced than freshmen. Also,
with very few exceptions, these differences are relatively large and are
statistically significant. Further, these differences are evident in such
diverse colleges and universities as the University of Santa Clara (a
Jesuit university in California), Bennington College (a small, select
liberal arts college for women on the East Coast), and Michigan State
University (a large, state multiversity in the Midwest). . . . In terms of
relatively consistent uniformities in net direction of change, some
changes that are characteristic of nearly all American colleges have
emerged. Most salient are increases in 'open-mindedness' (reflected by
declining authoritarianism, dogmatism, and prejudice), decreasing
conservatism in regard to public issues, and growing sensitivity to
aesthetic and 'inner' experiences" (Feldman and Newcomb, 1969, pp.
31, 48).

    Until much more research on this issue is accomplished, we
must conclude by agreeing with Feldman and Newcomb, who
stressed that the processes of selection are interdependent with the
processes of college impact (Feldman and Newcomb, 1969, pp. 333–
334). On the basis of our data, however, we predict future research will
disclose that educational process affects attitudes of political tolerance more than does educational selection.

Summary of Findings

    We found level of education to be strongly associated with
Stouffer's Tolerance Scale. This association was strong in 1954, but it
was much stronger in 1973. At the same time, the Tolerance
Scale scores associated with each educational level are greater in 1973
than in 1954; these increases are substantial for all educational groups
except those with only grade school training.

    Since the average level of education among the American
population has increased so dramatically in the past two decades, a
plausible interpretation of the rise in Tolerance Scale scores from
1954 to 1973 would be that this increase is a consequence of the
increase in level of education. Such an interpretation must be tempered, however, in light of differences in political climate at the time
of each study, for the sharp rise in the nation's educational level from

1954 to 1973 has been matched by a considerable decline in perceptions of Communist danger. This change in political climate has been shown to operate along with the increase in educational level in affecting increases in democratic restraint.

We found level of education to be distinct from occupational status in its impact on political tolerance. This finding supplies basic support for the idea that higher education affects political tolerance primarily through increasing people's cognitive skills, knowledge, and cultural sophistication. Many other analyses support this interpretation.

The participants in the 1973 study displaying by far the greatest support for civil liberties perceive little threat from Communism, score high on the Tolerance Scale, are highly educated, and are more politically competent and involved and hold less religiously orthodox views than other participants. All these analyses lend support to our view that the relationships between education and political tolerance are best interpreted as arising from the educational process rather than from education viewed as an indicator of social status or as a selection phenomenon or in terms of an acquiescent response-set.

The data presented in this chapter do not permit us to explain why the increase in Tolerance Scale scores from 1954 to 1973 was substantial within every educational grouping save the lowest one. Possibly some of this increase results from changes in the educational process itself, associated with what Trow (1966) called "the second transformation of American secondary education." The first half of this century was viewed by Trow as "the age of the terminal high school"; since World War II, in Trow's account, public sentiment has forced the public secondary school to transform itself into a mass preparatory system for the further education of its clients (Trow, 1966, pp. 438–441). We can suggest that the same "public sentiment" which underlies the transformation of the high schools is being manifested also in rising levels of tolerance, and that both transformations are rooted in the more basic metamorphosis of the American population from a relatively unschooled nation to a nation in which half the adult population has some schooling beyond high school. We can move beyond such speculation only with further data; the next chapter, focusing on differences in tolerance among persons of different age, provides additional facts essential for sifting reality from supposition.

Chapter 5

Age and
Political Tolerance

/\.\\/\\

A person's age is an intricate datum in social research. Information about chronological age is often used to sort people into age groups or to assemble them into birth cohorts for the purpose of describing trends through time. Various statistical maneuvers that yield decisions regarding the probable sources of observed trends subsequently may be carried out, such as the processes of growing older ("aging" or "maturational" sources), the experiences impinging on all the age groups over a given period of time ("historical" or "period" sources), or the experiences affecting only particular cohorts ("generational" or "cohort" sources). All these procedures, which are built up from the original datum of chronological age, display a solid, substantial, factual picture—a picture, nevertheless, that can be quite insubstantial and misleading.

Chronological age gains its meaning largely through being an index of important biological, social, or psychological experiences common to individuals (Bengtson and Black, 1973). But a root problem, revealed in Mannheim's seminal writings, is that chronological age as a sorting device may well aggregate individuals who have not undergone similar influences: "It is not difficult to see why mere chronological contemporaneity cannot of itself produce a common generation location. No one, for example, would assert that there was community of location between the young people of China and Germany about 1800" (Mannheim, 1964, p. 297). The point is illustrated with Berger's reference to our own recent past (1960, p. 28): "the proletarian decade dates also the emergence of the Southern Agrarian movement, conservative and anti-industrial; and, of course, Organization Men and 'suburbanites' coexist, indeed, even interact with the 'beat generation.'" Thus, although we focus on the relationship of age and tolerance in the discussion that follows, we have striven to avoid the misconstruction of reality that such a perspective can give. In this area we have found the ideas of Buss (1974), Glenn (1974), and Ryder (1965) especially useful.

Age Trends in Political Tolerance

A persistent notion among scholars and laymen alike is that people become more dogmatic and rigid in behavior and attitude as they grow older. The "fixation" model presented by Karlsson and Carlsson (1970, p. 71) stated the position directly: "With increasing age, people become less likely to change; in its later life, each birth cohort reflects, therefore, largely the conditions prevailing during its formative years." Similarly, Lambert (1972, p. 40) reasoned that "as the cumulation of experience, passing of time, and deterioration of brain, aging produces an increasingly stratified consciousness (more layers, elaboration, and rigidity or hardening of categories) and decelerating rate of socialization." However, much evidence from empirical research necessitates considerable modification of these views.

Assessing evidence on the general issue of behavioral change over the life span, Baltes and Schaie (1973, p. 369) observed that "marked behavioral change does occur at all age-levels, i.e., that life span change does indeed exist on the level of description." Reviews of studies in the area of political attitudes and behavior likewise offer little support to the aging/rigidity thesis. Foner (1974, p. 189) wrote: "Contrary to widespread assumptions about growing rigidity with age, certain studies . . . indicate that people do change political attitudes as they grow older, often becoming more liberal." Campbell's

(1971, p. 114) summary of national survey studies reached a similar judgment: "The one general conclusion which appears justified is that there is no simple relationship between age and political conservatism; generational differences are substantial in regard to some social and political issues but they are insignificant in regard to many others." Reviewing evidence regarding conservatism broadly conceived (including both political and social attitudes), Glenn (1974, p. 185) concluded that "according to almost any definition of conservatism, people have typically become less, rather than more, conservative as they have grown older, in conformity with general societal trends."

The "general societal trends" just noted are strong and pervasive, resulting in older people being relatively less conservative than during earlier periods of their own life histories yet being more conservative than younger persons in the population (Glenn, 1974, p. 185). These trends in attitudes of political and social conservatism are substantially reproduced in the case of political tolerance, to which we now turn.

First to be examined are two sets of responses portraying the extent of democratic restraint in 1954 and 1973. Table 19 arrays Toler-

Table 19. Age of Respondent and Score on Tolerance Scale,
National Cross Section, 1954 and 1973.

| Age | Tolerance Scale Scores: | | | |
	Percent Less Tolerant	Percent In-Between	Percent More Tolerant	Number
1954				
21 to 29	13	46	41	905
30 to 39	14	49	37	1,174
40 to 49	18	51	31	1,058
50 to 59	21	53	26	794
60 and older	22	62	16	998
1973				
21 to 29	5	19	76	740
30 to 39	9	26	65	660
40 to 49	14	30	56	591
50 to 59	18	36	46	552
60 and older	32	39	29	755

**Table 20. Age of Respondent and Disposition to Oppose Listening In on
Conversations of Suspected Communists, National Cross Section,
1954 and 1973.**

| | Percent Answering: | | | |
Age	Should Listen In	Should Not Listen In	No Opinion	Number
1954				
21 to 29	68	32		848
30 to 39	69	31		1,076
40 to 49	71	29		972
50 to 59	71	29		721
60 and older	75	25		896
1973				
21 to 29	36	61	3	737
30 to 39	43	53	4	660
40 to 49	47	49	4	591
50 to 59	52	44	4	551
60 and older	54	35	11	753

ance Scale scores by age of respondent for the two time periods; Table
20 displays dispositions to approve or to oppose listening in on the
telephone conversations of suspected Communists by age of respondent for the two time periods. In effect, these tables provide four snap-
shots of political tolerance in the United States; later in the chapter,
these and other data will be assembled into birth cohort groups to
reveal more clearly the ongoing, dynamic patterns of change in political tolerance as persons grow older.

The results given in Tables 19 and 20 indicate that politically
tolerant responses are more prevalent among younger persons than
among older persons, both in 1954 and in 1973. A second important
result common to both measures of political tolerance is that the gap
between the youngest and the oldest age groups in the proportion
endorsing democratic restraint is wider in 1973 than in 1954. With
respect to Tolerance Scale results, for example, Table 19 shows that
the gap between the youngest and oldest age groups in 1954 was 25
percentage points (41 compared with 16 percent more tolerant); in
1973, 47 percentage points separate the youngest and oldest age
groups (76 compared with 29 percent more tolerant). For convenience
of reference, these percentage-point differences are given in Table 21.

Table 21. Percentage Points by Which the Youngest Age Group Exceeds the Oldest Age Group in Endorsing Politically Tolerant Responses, 1954 and 1973.

Year	Tolerance Scale	Listening In on Communists
1954	25	7
1973	47	26

The import of these data is that, although persons at all age levels became more politically tolerant during the period 1954 to 1973, the upsurge in tolerance was markedly greater for younger persons than for older persons. For the present, it is convenient to note and set aside this remarkable outcome with only the comment that these findings are identical in pattern with the results summarized by Glenn (1974) on relations between age and conservative political and social attitudes, as discussed earlier. The matter of youth and political tolerance is explored in some detail toward the end of this chapter.

Education and Age Trends in Political Tolerance

As a first step toward explaining associations between age groupings and political tolerance, it is useful to recall the discussion in Chapter Four of the sharply accelerated educational upgrading within the American population over the past two decades. Perhaps the age differences in political tolerance just observed come about mainly through the greater education of younger, as compared with older, persons in 1973. If this hypothesis were true, then similar expressions of democratic restraint should occur among persons of the same level of education, no matter what their age. The data presented in Table 22 on Tolerance Scale scores, age group, and level of education are ambiguous regarding this hypothesis; data (not presented) for other measures of political tolerance yield the same patterns. Contrary to the hypothesis, the table shows a systematic trend for younger persons to score more tolerant than older persons *at each level of education*. As an example, following the percentage scoring more tolerant among high school graduates across the age groups in Table 22, one finds a steady decline from 72 percent for those in their twenties, to 63 percent for those in their thirties, to 53 percent for

Table 22. Age, Education, and Score on Tolerance Scale, 1973.

		Tolerance Scale Scores:			
Age in 1973	Level of Education	Percent Less Tolerant	Percent In- Between	Percent More Tolerant	Number
21 to 29	College graduate	2	5	93	166
	Some college	2	14	84	202
	High school	5	23	72	244
	Some high school	17	32	52	79
	Grade school	15	51	33	39
30 to 39	College graduate	1	10	89	132
	Some college	4	15	82	103
	High school	10	27	63	251
	Some high school	16	44	40	107
	Grade school	22	40	38	60
40 to 49	College graduate	4	12	84	106
	Some college	5	24	71	96
	High school	16	31	53	197
	Some high school	20	38	43	120
	Grade school	30	49	21	67
50 to 59	College graduate	8	15	77	61
	Some college	12	24	64	78
	High school	15	34	51	178
	Some high school	16	47	37	124
	Grade school	35	48	17	99
60 and older	College graduate	10	25	65	80
	Some college	24	26	50	76
	High school	20	43	37	136
	Some high school	32	42	26	134
	Grade school	45	42	14	321

those in their forties, to 51 percent for those in their fifties, and to a low of 37 percent for those sixty or older. Of the twenty such comparisons possible, eighteen show declines in tolerance score with age.

These results indicate that the greater political tolerance expressed by younger persons in comparison with older persons must arise in part for reasons other than the higher education levels that exist among young people; at the same time, however, the data in Table 22 show the strong relationship between level of education and political tolerance among persons at all age levels. This strong relationship can be highlighted by adopting the idea of the "effectiveness" of education used by Hyman, Wright, and Reed (1975, pp. 54–55): "Each gain in absolute percentage points when expressed in terms of its ratio to the maximum gain that is possible over the level of knowledge [in this study, over the level of political tolerance] exhibited by the less-educated group yields the index of effectiveness and translates the absolute gain into a relative or standardized measure."

To illustrate, consider the effectiveness in promoting political tolerance of a high school education as compared with a grade school education among persons in their twenties. Table 22 shows that among persons in their twenties with grade school education, 33 percent score more tolerant. Thus, the maximum gain possible in political tolerance given increased education among persons in this age group would be 67 percent. The table shows that 72 percent of high school graduates in their twenties score more tolerant, an increase of 39 percentage points over the grade school group. Dividing this figure by the maximum possible increase of 67 percent (39/67) and multiplying by 100 yields the Index of Educational Effectiveness number in this case, which is 58. The figure may be interpreted as follows: other things being equal, among persons in their twenties in 1973, having a high school education produced a gain in political tolerance that was 58 percent of the maximum gain possible, given the level of political tolerance among the least-educated group.

Three series of indexes as computed from the data of Table 22 are shown in Table 23. Although the figures are meant to be illustrative, and by no means are they meant to establish the precise contribution of education to political tolerance, the reader can appreciate more readily here than in Table 22 the somewhat different effects of

Table 23. Indexes of Educational Effectiveness in Raising Tolerance Scale Scores (Percent Scoring More Tolerant) Among Different Age Groups, 1973.

Age in 1973	High School Versus Grade School Graduate	College Versus High School Graduate	College Versus Grade School Graduate
21 to 29	58	75	90
30 to 39	40	70	82
40 to 49	41	66	80
50 to 59	40	53	72
60 and older	27	44	59

education among the different age groups. In particular, as one reads down the columns of the table, the greater impact of education on tolerance among young persons in comparison with older persons is revealed; as one reads across the rows of the table, the increasing impact of higher amounts of education on tolerance within each of the age groups is revealed.

Birth Cohorts and Political Tolerance

Thus far we have been trying to understand how political tolerance is related to age by discussing results for persons aggregated into age groups at two particular periods: 1954 and 1973. We now approach the problem from the standpoint of the procession of generations, in which waves of birth cohorts reach adulthood, succeed older cohorts as responsible, maturing generations, and ultimately disappear from the population through death.

In this analysis, it is essential to keep in mind certain characteristics of the information at hand. First, data were not gathered from the same persons in 1954 and 1973, so the findings will lack the full force that would arise from having measures for the same individuals at two points in time. However, since the 1973 study was planned as a replication of the 1954 study, much information is available that was elicited through identically worded questions. Similarly, the samples for the two studies were developed through strict probability procedures designed to provide representative samples of the noninstitutionalized adult population of the United States. Thus, even though measures for the same people at two points in time are lacking, the common sampling procedures used in 1954 and 1973, coupled with the identical measures employed, may be viewed as providing highly reliable data for estimating change.

There is an advantage to studying birth cohorts after a time lapse of nearly two decades; such a span of time is long enough to allow for the emergence of substantial period effects—outcomes due to events occurring in the interval between the two studies—if such effects, indeed, have accumulated. From the standpoint of tracing birth cohort effects (or effects within generations defined by criteria other than birth), however, the fact that nineteen years elapsed between studies means that results for nearly a third of the 1954 respondents will be essentially uninterpretable. That is, the persons aged fifty and older in 1954 will have become sixty-nine years old and older by 1973; attrition due to senility, institutionalization, and death will have changed the characteristics of the surviving group, transforming it into a biased sample of its original birth cohort.* For these reasons, the cohort analysis considers only persons who were less than fifty years of age in 1954.

A final constraint of the birth cohort analysis is that the 1954 age data are available only in collapsed form, that is, for persons in their twenties, thirties, forties, fifties, and sixty years old or older. The birth cohorts used, then, are the narrowest ones it is possible to establish, given the time between the two studies and the grouped nature of the age data for the persons studied in 1954.

Table 24 presents two measures of political tolerance, in 1954

Table 24. Birth Cohorts and Political Tolerance, 1954 and 1973.

Born in:	Age in:		Tolerance Scale: Percent More Tolerant			Listening In on Conversations: Percent Should Not		
	1954	1973	1954	1973	Change	1954	1973	Change
1925– 1933	21–29	40–48	41	56	+15	32	49	+17
1915– 1924	30–39	49–58	37	48	+11	31	45	+14
1905– 1914	40–49	59–68	31	33	+2	29	35	+6

and 1973, among persons in the three youngest birth cohorts of the 1954 study. Because the two measures of political tolerance being used —the percentage scoring more tolerant on the Tolerance Scale and the percentage opposing listening in on Communists—provide somewhat different estimates of democratic restraint at the two time

*For identical reasons, Hyman, Wright, and Reed (1975, pp. 31–32, 298) set the upper bounds of their age groups at age seventy-two. Because the 1954 age data were available only by decades of life, we had the choice of setting the upper bound either at age sixty-eight (persons who were in their forties in 1954) or at age seventy-eight (persons who were in their fifties in 1954).

points, any consistent patterns of change for both measures should add to one's confidence that real changes in democratic restraint have occurred. It may be noted first that the data in Table 24 provide no support for the idea that growing older brings about lowered political tolerance. The table shows increases in tolerance for each birth cohort on both of the measures. This outcome is impressive, since it occurs not only among persons moving from young adulthood to early maturity (those in their twenties in 1954) but also among persons moving from the middle years of adulthood to the full-fledged maturity of the retirement years. These trends invite the implication that factors at work during the period of 1954 to 1973 raised the level of political tolerance across the wide range of the adult population being studied here; these historical or period effects are examined further below.

Another pattern in the results of Table 24 strongly suggests the operation of cohort effects, of differences arising, that is, from differences existing prior to 1954 between cohorts. The propensity to increase in political tolerance from 1954 to 1973 is clearly greater for the two younger birth cohorts than for the older cohort. A potential source of these cohort effects, of course, is differential educational levels among the three birth cohorts. Although the discussion in Chapter Four stressed that education levels rose dramatically between 1954 and 1973, such changes could not have involved many of the persons in the cohorts being studied, since most of these persons would have completed their formal schooling before 1954. An appreciation of the educational differences experienced by these persons, however, can be gained by examining United States census data. Table 25

**Table 25. Median School Years Completed
by Americans in Recent Decades.**

Year	Persons 25 Years Old and Over	Persons 25 Years Old and Over
1940	10.3	8.6
1950	12.1	9.3
1960	12.3	9.9
1970	12.6	12.2
1972	12.7	12.3

Source: U.S. Bureau of the Census (1974, Table 186, p. 116).

shows the educational changes that have been transforming America. The 1940 figures roughly characterize the educational experience of the oldest birth cohort, whose members were twenty-six to thirty-five years old in 1940; the 1950 figures crudely indicate the educational experience of the next oldest cohort, whose members were twenty-six to thirty-five years old in 1950; and the 1960 figures give a loose approximation of the educational experience of the youngest cohort, whose members were twenty-seven to thirty-five years old in 1960.

The educational levels of the two younger birth cohorts (estimated by the 1950 and 1960 figures in Table 25) are at once highly similar to one another and abruptly disjunctive with the educational level for the oldest birth cohort (estimated by the 1940 figures in Table 25). Many persons in the two younger cohorts are members of the first birth cohorts in American society to register half their members as high school graduates or more.

Because of the rather loose fit between the decennial census data and our birth cohorts, the actual educational distributions as reported by the persons interviewed in 1954 and in 1973 were also studied. Both the 1954 and the 1973 estimates showed the same basic facts as the census figures: there is a distinct disjunction in educational experience between the two younger birth cohorts and the older birth cohort, the younger groups displaying sharply higher proportions with higher amounts of education. These educational differences are a plausible source of the birth cohort differences in democratic restraint established thus far.

Having developed a case for the birth cohort effects shown in Table 24, let us return now to discussion of potential factors at work during the period of 1954 to 1973 that might underlie the general rise in political tolerance observed for all three birth cohorts. Recall the discussion in Chapter Three: a whole series of events occurred between 1954 and 1973 that resulted in a diminution in perceived Communist threat. Another, much more complex set of influences, discussed in terms of educational change in Chapter Four, is highlighted again by the data of Table 25. The table shows that the young adults in 1950 entered a society which was much less educated, on the average, than was their own age group. By 1972, this circumstance was altered to the point that the young people entering the adult world averaged less than half a grade level above the median schooling for the adult population generally. In terms of the educational levels spreading throughout the adult population by the time of our study in 1973, the society truly had been transformed since 1954.

The educational metamorphosis taking place in our society is itself but one of many changes leading toward a qualitatively new organization of life. In Bell's (1973, pp. 167–174) account of the "post-industrial society," the concepts of the "pace of change" (often exponential) and the "change of scale" (massive) convey the flavor of the modern world as it is experienced by contemporary adults. Within the context of a society that is by normative tradition and institutional arrangement a political democracy, the intensification of new experiences among an ever-more-educated and urbanized population should call forth many new occasions for the practice of democratic restraint. Such are the forces at work, then, that should accumulate as a "period effect" uplifting the levels of political tolerance among the birth cohorts under study.

A statistical test establishing unambiguously the existence and extent of the cohort and the period effects we have been discussing is not possible because, as we noted at the beginning of the chapter, effects associated with these two sources are confounded with effects attributable to aging. However, if one is willing to assume that the process of aging is unimportant for political tolerance, it is possible to test for the effects of birth cohorts and historical periods. This assumption seems a reasonable one to make, on two grounds: (1) the review of evidence from other studies and the present one discredited the idea that aging in itself has important effects on political tolerance; (2) cogent empirical and theoretical reasons were advanced above for expecting both cohort and period effects.

Table 26 provides a test for the relative effects associated with birth cohorts and historical period, following the cross-sequential method shown as appropriate for independent random samples by Schaie and Strother (1968). The table shows that the hypothesized effects arising both from differences in birth cohorts and from historical factors are statistically significant beyond the .001 level of probability. In addition, the significant "cohort X time" interaction means that the historical effect cannot be generalized to all three cohorts nor the cohort effect generalized across both time periods. Essentially what is emerging is a similar upward shift in Tolerance Scale scores

Table 26. Cross-Sequential Analysis of Variance of Tolerance Scale Scores,
Selected Birth Cohorts, 1954 and 1973.

Age in 1954	Mean Tolerance for Birth Cohorts:		
	Time 1 1954	Time 2 1973	Average Over Times
21 to 29	3.12	3.49	3.25
30 to 39	2.95	3.21	3.04
40 to 49	2.74	2.63	2.71
Average over cohorts	2.93	3.15	3.00

Source of Variance	Sum of Squares	D.F.	Mean Square	F-ratios	F
Cohorts	206.67	2	103.34	45.67	.001
Time of measurement	35.67	1	35.67	15.76	.001
Cohort X time interaction	39.90	2	19.95	8.82	.001
Residual	10,498.89	4,640	2.26		
Total variance	10,794.10	4,645	2.32		

among the two younger birth cohorts through time, a trend that is not
shared with the third birth cohort. These results clearly support the
account we have given of age-related factors affecting the different
birth cohort groups through time.

Youth and Political Tolerance

The idea of "fresh contact" developed by Mannheim (1964, pp.
293–294) provides a helpful beginning for understanding the soaring
levels of political tolerance expressed by the majority of younger
Americans today: "In the nature of our psychical make-up, a fresh
contact (meeting something anew) always means a changed relationship of distance from the object and a novel approach in assimilating,
using, and developing the proffered material. . . . The continuous
emergence of new human beings certainly results in some loss of
accumulated cultural possessions; but, on the other hand, it alone
makes a fresh selection possible when it becomes necessary; it facili-
tates reevaluation of our inventory and teaches us both to forget that
which is no longer useful and to covet that which has yet to be won."

Consider in this light the persons in their twenties and thirties in 1973, all of whom were too young for inclusion in the birth cohort analysis just completed. Such persons are distinguished from older Americans by having grown up during the post–World War II years. Even the thirty-nine-year-olds in the 1973 study, who were born as long ago as 1934, were preadolescents in 1945. In terms of experience germane to political tolerance, then, what was involved in "fresh contact" with the world in the United States after World War II?

Confronting the post-1945 world "anew" meant experiencing the exhilarating "pace of change" and massive "change of scale" associated with those years as merely ordinary; it meant that being a well-educated person was commonplace, and that the *experience* of being a highly educated member of an educationally advanced society —surely a unique feature of the post-1945 world—was routine; it meant that living in cities amid many other persons and groups, all expressing a multiplicity of values, was the rule; and it meant that working alongside and in cooperation with tens, hundreds, and even thousands of other persons in large-scale organizations was one's everyday, unexceptional lot.

It must be remembered that these contemporary conditions of complexity, diversity, and change are occurring among a people whose traditions of political democracy are not only securely intact but actively promoted at home,* in school, and in the mass media. A leading student of American values, for example, in discussing changes in values that might help explain the sharp decline in anti-Semitism in the years following World War II, wrote: "Since the

---

*We do not mean to suggest that children are highly similar to their parents in political and social attitudes; rather, the evidence indicates strong attitudinal similarities between parental and child *generations*. Connell's review of parent-child studies concluded that "processes within the family have been largely irrelevant to the formation of specific opinions. It appears that older and younger generations have developed their opinions in parallel rather than in series, by similar experiences in a common world. . . . That children may gain from their parents some idea of the range of acceptable opinions is quite likely. That specific opinions generally come with mother's milk is—for America, 1944–1968—rather decisively disproved" (1972, p. 330). Even more recently, Bengtson (1975, p. 369), after assessing data over three generations, concluded that: "the findings of this study suggest neither (a) marked generational differences nor (b) strong familial similarity in value orientations."

1930s, American society as a whole has increasingly acknowledged a public obligation to guard, nurture, and care for various types of disadvantaged or unfortunate persons: women, children, Negroes, the unemployed, the destitute, the physically or emotionally ill, the victims of disaster. This deepening concern reflects the values of *humanitarianism,* or regard for the individual personality, of *freedom,* and of *equality"* (Williams, 1966, p. 347).

On the basis of both the changed social conditions described previously and these deepening value commitments, it is reasonable that persons in fresh contact with American life after World War II would take as their own the attitudes and behaviors constituting democratic restraint. But we must add to these general social and cultural factors the specific stimulation arising from the tumultuous decade of the 1960s. Altbach and Kelly (1973, pp. 24–25) assessed the importance of the civil rights movement for youth during the early part of the decade as follows: "Indeed it was the civil liberties issue which first aroused student concern after the political quiet of the 1950s. . . . The civil rights movement became the most important focus of student activism after the decline of the peace movement around 1963 and succeeded in attracting unprecedented student support (since the 1930s at least), and touched an important element in the society at large. The early sit-ins and nonviolent civil rights activities, particularly in the South, brought a sense of national urgency to the issue of race relations and had an impact in terms of national legislation and public opinion."

If the civil rights issue rallied a minority of college students and other youth in the early part of the 1960s, in the process bringing questions of political tolerance to the forefront of the developing consciousness of all young people, the latter half of the decade came to be dominated by the Vietnam War. Every observer—and they were legion*—viewed the war in Vietnam as being the most fundamental influence among the young during the sixties. For many young persons, the war raised moral and political sensibilities to a level of

---

*In the words of Altbach and Kelly (1973, p. 1): "Even on the relatively limited topic of student activism it is not possible to provide a complete analysis of the literature. The scope of materials has grown so much in the late sixties that a full discussion of all relevant studies is an almost impossible task."

intensity, sustained throughout the latter half of the decade, that forged deep attachments to humanitarian concerns in general and to the issues comprehended by political tolerance in particular.

Assuredly there were other influences, prominent among them an animosity toward existing authority. In its extreme form, rioting, this animosity denied the legitimacy of political tolerance; in its milder versions, political cynicism or indifference, it denied the utility of political tolerance. Alongside all the activities of the latter 1960s was the romantic elevation of the individual's claims to dignity, indulgence, and personal fruition above the society's demands for order, allegiance, and disciplined toil (Shils, 1969).

Several studies in addition to the present one assess evidence concerning age and politically relevant attitudes. A dramatic demonstration of the impact on youth of the Vietnam War was provided by Erskine's (1972-73, p. 616) review of 185 opinion poll items regarding war and pacifism in studies conducted from 1936 to the early 1970s: "Before the mid-60s youthful America was actually more likely to subscribe to aggressive world patterns. Their seniors most opposed warlike behavior on the part of the United States in 62 percent of the questions. Ever since the Vietnam controversy became heated, however, the young have outvoted their elders on the side of peace three-quarters of the time."

In contrast to the cohort effect Erskine described, Cutler and Bengtson's (1974, p. 172) analysis of national sample data regarding political alienation in 1952, 1960, and 1968, although finding younger birth cohorts less politically alienated than older ones, stresses the importance of a period effect common to all the cohorts: "The data for the whole sample . . . dramatically indicate that for these measures of political alienation, all of the generational cohorts responded to the stimuli of 1952 to 1968 in an almost identical fashion. No matter what the starting level of political alienation in 1952, it was followed by a drop in 1960 and, then, an upsurge in 1968. Thus, it may be concluded that although each successive cohort evidences slightly lower levels of alienation, there is only slight evidence that patterns of political alienation in the United States across the years 1952 to 1968 can be usefully interpreted in generational terms."

Still a third pattern of age-related evidence was reported by Fischer (1974), in a very thorough birth cohort analysis of Detroit

Area Study data on social alienation for the years 1958 to 1971. Although she acknowledged that "anomia increased relatively uniformly within all cohorts" (p. 39), she went on to emphasize the striking effects among the young (pp. 88–89): "On one point the evidence seems clear. Membership in the new cohort in 1971 has a consistently alienating effect. We find evidence of a 'cohort chasm' between those over and under thirty-five in 1971, although the discontinuity is blurred by the effects of intercohort educational differences. The relatively high level of anomia among youthful respondents in 1971 does not appear to be an effect of youth per se, but rather an effect of membership in the cohort born after 1935. The common exposure to the frustrations of the Vietnam War may account for the disenchantment of this group of young people."

If all the results just reviewed are valid, then we may describe post-World War II youth as more antiwar, less alienated politically, and more anomic or socially alienated than older generations.* Each outcome can be considered plausible on the basis of one or more of the social conditions and cultural values experienced uniquely by them in the post-World War II world. At the same time, no one outcome seems to us to be as compelling as do the results of the present study, in which young persons in their twenties and thirties in 1973 exhibit markedly higher levels of democratic restraint than do older persons. In sum, the fit between societal complexity, diversity, and change, on the one hand, and the emergence of extensive support for traditional civil liberties among the young, on the other hand, seems to us remarkably snug.

The discussion of youth and political tolerance has stressed Mannheim's idea of the importance of experiencing the world naively, for the first time. It is possible to give a pertinent example of this process. Recall that the degree of perception of a Communist threat diminished in our society between 1954 and 1973. This being so,

---

*The studies just reviewed are among the few relevant birth cohort studies based on large and reliable samples. Many useful studies based on special samples or data gathered at only one time are found in Bengtson and Laufer (1974). The series of national sample studies carried out by Yankelovich (1974) provide helpful cross-sectional data concerning this quite young age group. Inglehart (1971) presented an analysis of European data that is consistent with age trends we have reported.

Table 27. Age and Perception of a Serious Communist Threat,
1954 and 1973.

Age Groups	1954: Percent	1954: Number	1973: Percent	1973: Number
21 to 29	47	905	20	740
30 to 39	41	1,174	28	660
40 to 49	43	1,098	32	591
50 to 59	44	794	35	552
60 and older	42	998	33	755

younger persons in 1973, experiencing the world anew, should express less concern about Communism than older persons, who may carry forward some residue of concern from the past. The data in Table 27 show the indicated patterns. In the society of 1954, perception of a threat from Communism was more uniform and relatively high among persons of all ages. In the society of 1973, although perception of a Communist threat had diminished appreciably for persons of all ages, the younger persons (especially those in their twenties) were noticeably less likely to perceive Communism as a serious threat than were the older persons.

In considering the question of generational differences within a systematic exposition of social change, Katz (1974) reasoned that age does not provide a solid base for *societal* change; age confers only a fleeting status. Changes in the social arrangements by which rewards are distributed among people require a less ephemeral source of power. *Cultural* changes, as in "habits of dress, types of music, sexual practices, and mores" (Katz, 1974, p. 173) are, however, viewed as likely outcomes of age-cohort interaction. Given these distinctions, Katz then raised an important question: "The question that needs more research is whether this cultural change has seriously modified the values which legitimate social and political institutions. The significant outcome of generational differences may be not a radically new set of values but an acceleration of an existing trend, namely the refusal to equate authority and existing practices with morality."

The present data bear directly on this question, for we have found that young Americans have embraced a received and quite basic American political tradition—the attitudes and practices involved in democratic restraint and political tolerance—in unprece-

Table 28. Age and Expression of Politically Tolerant
Responses to Seven Questions About Civil Liberties, 1973.

| | Percent Giving Politically Tolerant Response to: | | |
Age in 1973	None to Three Questions	Four to Seven Questions	Number
21 to 29	49	51	740
30 to 39	57	43	660
40 to 49	62	38	591
50 to 59	63	37	552
60 and older	74	26	755

dented numbers. Additional data arising from seven other questions
regarding civil liberties asked in the 1973 study (Table 28) reveal once
again the extraordinary tendency for younger Americans to lead all
others in expressing politically tolerant views. The cultural legacy of
democratic restraint is most prevalent among the young.

Age and the Future of Political Tolerance

Many results discussed in this chapter hold out the promise of
uninterrupted growth in political tolerance during the decades
ahead. It seems likely that the pace of change, the societal complexity,
and the diversity of life styles, which, we believe, joined in elevating
the level of political tolerance from 1954 to 1973, will persist. The
level of education in the society must continue to rise, as the highly
educated youth of today replace the lesser educated older cohorts. By
1990, according to Neugarten (1974), half of the persons aged fifty-
five to seventy-four will have a high school education or better.
Indeed, the prospects for intense political involvement on the part of
these aging cohorts are very high, in Neugarten's judgment (p. 197):
"These are parents of school-aged children at the time when the public schools are being challenged to provide better outcomes for disadvantaged groups and when the issues of desegregation and busing
have become personal issues. . . . Furthermore, they have come into
political maturity in an age when persons look increasingly to government—whether federal or local—not only to provide essential services and to protect citizens from harm, but also to improve the qual-

ity of their lives. These experiences and these attitudes, combined with their higher educational and occupational levels, will probably lead the future young-old to exert a potent influence on government."

Yet not quite all the data we have assessed presage the infusion of the national life with an excess of democratic restraint. When the youngest and most highly educated birth cohort in 1973 contains a majority who believe it is a "good idea" to report suspected Communists to the FBI, as well as containing more than one third who approve of listening in on the telephone conversations of suspected Communists, ample room for further cultivating attitudes of political tolerance is clearly available. Given a realistic menace to domestic tranquility enduring over a length of time, the swelling upward trend in support for civil liberties toward which most signs now point might well subside.

Chapter 6

Geographical Region, Size of Residential Area, and Political Tolerance

/\.\

The historical migration of Americans from sparsely settled rural areas to more densely inhabited urban areas continued during the years between the 1954 and 1973 studies. From 1950 to 1970, the proportion of the population classified as rural by the U.S. Census Bureau declined from 36 to 26.5 percent, with the proportion classified as urban rising accordingly from 64 to 73.5 percent. Although it is true that the proportion of Americans residing in metropolises of a million or more people actually declined over this time period (from 11.5 percent of the population in 1950 to 9.2 percent in 1970), the move from large cities was not to the open country but to suburbs, to cities of smaller size, or to densely populated though unincorporated outlying areas (U.S. Bureau of the Census, 1975, Table 20, p. 19).

Accompanying the growing concentration of population in urban areas has been a steeper rise in political tolerance among persons in cities than among persons living in smaller towns or on farms. Tables 29 and 30 show, first, that both in 1954 and in 1973 the politically tolerant responses are endorsed more frequently by persons liv-

Table 29. Size of Current Place of Residence and
Political Tolerance, National Cross Section, 1954 and 1973.

Size of Place of Residence	Tolerance Scale Scores:			
	Percent Less Tolerant	Percent In-Between	Percent More Tolerant	Number
1954				
100,000 or more	14	47	39	1,891
2,500 to 99,999	21	49	30	1,363
Under 2,500	22	53	25	917
Farm	30	53	17	762
				4,933
1973				
100,000 or more	9	25	66	1,634
2,500 to 99,999	19	30	51	1,078
Under 2,500	22	36	42	713
Farm	31	39	30	121
				3,546

Table 30. Size of Current Place of Residence and Disposition to
Oppose Listening In on Conversations of
Suspected Communists, 1954 and 1973.

Size of Place of Residence	Percent Answering:		
	Should Listen In	Should Not Listen In	Number
1954			
100,000 or more	66	34	1,726
2,500 to 99,999	70	30	1,258
Under 2,500	77	23	847
Farm	76	24	678
			4,509
1973			
100,000 or more	42	58	1,566
2,500 to 99,999	53	47	1,011
Under 2,500	53	47	672
Farm	54	46	113
			3,362

ing in areas of high population, but the more important result is that
the *increases* in the percentage of tolerant responses from 1954 to 1973
are greater in the larger than in the smaller residential areas.

The trend toward a greater disparity in political tolerance between persons living in cities and those living in rural areas is summarized in Table 31. In terms of the Tolerance Scale, for example, the

Table 31. Percentage Points by Which Persons Living in Large Cities Exceed Persons Living on Farms in Endorsing Politically Tolerant Responses, 1954 and 1973.

Year	Tolerance Scale	Listening In on Communists
1954	22	10
1973	36	12

table shows that in 1954, the difference in the proportion classified as more tolerant in large cities than on farms was 22 percentage points; by 1973, this difference had grown to 36 percentage points.

The continuing and expanding differences in political tolerance between persons residing in places of differing size attest to the abiding heterogeneity of opinion, rather than to a "massification" of outlook, among Americans. Other recent studies support this conclusion. Glenn and Alston (1967, pp. 384, 393), after summarizing results from national sample surveys conducted over the period 1953 to 1965, reported: "If we accept the responses at their face value, the farmers are unambiguously less informed, more prejudiced, less favorable to civil liberties, less tolerant of deviance, more ethnocentric and isolationist, more work-oriented and ascetic, more puritanical, less favorable to birth control, less trusting of people, and more favorable to early marriage and high fertility than most or all categories of urban workers." Equally impressive documentation of attitudinal differences along urban-rural lines comes from a Pennsylvania study of traditional moral attitudes among high school students. Analyzing data collected in 1947, 1960, and 1970 from sophomores in seventy-four Pennsylvania high schools, Willets, Bealer, and Crider (1973, pp. 42–43) found a general trend away from traditional moral attitudes "toward a more liberal or permissive position in 1970." These authors concluded that: "What can be said presently is that, mass society theorists notwithstanding, the leveling of residence differences was not found in the present data. On the contrary, residence appeared to be more useful in 1970 than it was 10 or 20 years earlier...."

Table 32. Size of Place of Residence at Age 16 and Score on Tolerance Scale, 1973.

| | Tolerance Scale Scores: | | | |
Size of Place of Residence	Percent Less Tolerant	Percent In-Between	Percent More Tolerant	Number
100,000 or more	8	25	68	892
Suburb near a city of 100,000 or more	5	18	77	342
City or town less than 100,000	15	29	56	1,170
Open country but not farm	19	29	52	389
Farm	27	42	31	745
				3,538

In other words, the more rural residents were not without some changes, but they evidenced relative lags in their willingness to depart from traditional attitudinal positions. As a result, the distinctions among the residence groupings have increased."

Finally, marked rural-urban differences in attitudes regarding civil rights among a national sample of Presbyterian ministers and lay leaders were reported by Nelsen and Yokley (1970, p. 167): "Excluding respondents who failed to answer one or more of the questions comprising the scale, we found that one-fifth of the rural respondents scored at the positive end of the scale compared to not quite half of the large city respondents."

In addition to information on current place of residence, participants in the 1973 study were asked the size of the places in which they were living when they were sixteen years old. When the 1973 study members are so categorized, their Tolerance Scale scores (Table 32) and attitudes about wiretapping suspected Communists' telephones (Table 33) are found to vary in a fashion almost identical with that already observed among persons classified by their current places of residence. Again, a persisting similarity of response among persons classified by their early and their current places of residence is shown in Table 34, which summarizes answers to seven questions about civil liberties asked in the 1973 study. Evidently, both growing up in places

**Table 33. Size of Place of Residence at Age 16 and Disposition
to Oppose Listening In on Conversations of
Suspected Communists, 1973.**

Size of Place of Residence	*Percent Answering:*		
	Should Listen In	*Should Not Listen In*	*Number*
100,000 or more	38	62	856
Suburb near a city of 100,000 or more	40	60	328
City or town less than 100,000	49	51	1,122
Open country but not farm	51	49	364
Farm	61	39	685
			3,355

**Table 34. Size of Place of Residence and Expression of Politically Tolerant
Responses to Seven Questions About Civil Liberties, 1973.**

Size of Place of Residence	*Percent Giving Politically Tolerant Response to:*		
	None to Three Questions	*Four to Seven Questions*	*Number*
Current			
100,000 or more	54	46	1,634
2,500 to 99,999	65	35	1,078
Under 2,500	67	33	713
Farm	68	32	121
			3,546
At age 16			
100,000 or more	51	49	892
Suburb near a city of 100,000 or more	50	50	342
City or town less than 100,000	61	39	1,170
Open country but not farm	64	36	389
Farm	73	27	745
			3,538

of larger size and current residence in such places promote expression of politically tolerant attitudes.

If it is clear that enduring differences in political tolerance exist among Americans living in places of different size, the relative importance of various factors affecting this outcome is less clear. The main problem is in separating effects arising from specific city characteristics—such as large size, heterogeneity of population, and dense concentrations of people—from effects arising out of differences in individual characteristics (such as education level) between persons living in larger and smaller places. For example, if the average education of persons living in smaller places were identical with that of persons living in larger cities, would city dwellers continue to show higher proportions of tolerant people? In a recent study, part of an ongoing series of careful researches on this general question, Fischer (1975a, p. 431) concluded that "urban residence per se has small but real effects on adherence to traditional values. That is, urban-rural variations in individual characteristics do not completely explain the urban-deviance association." Analyses of the 1954 and 1973 data controlling for effects of education, region, exposure to mass media, gender, and occupation have likewise reported persisting relations between political tolerance and size of place of residence (Williams, Nunn, and St. Peter, 1976a).

A general theory of incongruent experience proposed by Borhek (1965, p. 89) is useful in understanding how size of place of residence may help bring about increased tolerance: "The theory of incongruent experience states that the tendency to think in black and white terms and to reduce issues to oversimplifications is a result of individuals having been exposed to backgrounds which were impoverished in terms of ideas, or in having lacked either direct or vicarious exposure to other ways of life and other ways of defining situations. We propose that tolerance, on the other hand, is the result of experiences which are characterized by heterogeneity of ideas or direct or vicarious exposure to other ways of life and other ways of defining situations." Increases in size of place should raise a person's likelihood of encountering new ideas and situations and hence expand the alternatives of thought and action of which he is aware; such a variety of experience reduces the likelihood of "unquestioned commitment to any ideology, group, or set of norms" (Borhek, 1965, p. 93) and in so doing enhances the likelihood of political tolerance.

Region and Political Tolerance

With modern systems of rapid communication and transportation bringing people living in different states into daily commerce
with each other both culturally (through the news media) and eco-
nomically (through the marketplace), and with a steady, nationwide
trend creating a predominantly urban population, the concept of
region as a tool for social research has been neglected and nearly dis-
carded. There is, to be sure, continued perfunctory use by many
researchers of the U.S. Census Bureau's standard groupings of the
states into broad geographical regions, so that readers are familiar
with information presented under the labels West, East, Midwest, and
South. But the use of region to denote something more than contigu-
ous geographical location is today little known. Yet only twenty-five
years ago the concept of regionalism was still vital as a means of
understanding American society, so Vance could write (1951, p. 123):
"Each region must differ from neighboring regions but must
approximate a mode of homogeneous characteristics if it is to possess
identity. As an objective entity and as a heuristic device for research,
the ideal region will always be the composite region in which economic, political, and cultural identity is evident. Since part of this
will inhere in the nature of the data and part will inhere in the purpose of the investigator, we are likely to have continued controversies
about the structure and functions of specific regions."

Although in following Stouffer's 1954 procedure we are using
the standard U.S. Census Bureau regional classifications,* we remain
open to the possibility that more robust meanings than mere location
endure as part of the idea of region. Indeed, although using the broad
census categories, Glenn and Simmons' (1967, p. 187) analysis of
national survey data collected as recently as the 1960s concluded: "If
the differences by age indicate trends, and if large sampling errors

---

*The regions are *West:* Washington, Oregon, California, Idaho,
Nevada, Montana, Wyoming, Utah, Arizona, Colorado, New Mexico; *East:*
Maine, New Hampshire, Vermont, Massachusetts, Rhode Island, Connecti-
cut, New York, New Jersey, Pennsylvania; *Midwest:* Ohio, Michigan,
Indiana, Illinois, Wisconsin, Minnesota, Iowa, Missouri, North Dakota,
South Dakota, Nebraska, Kansas; *South:* Maryland, Delaware, District of
Columbia, Virginia, West Virginia, North Carolina, South Carolina,
Georgia, Alabama, Arkansas, Florida, Kentucky, Louisiana, Mississippi,
Oklahoma, Tennessee, Texas.

were not unusually numerous, the regions have *diverged* in most of the attitudes covered by this study that relate to personal morality, the relative desirability of occupations, racial and ethnic minorities, international relations, and political issues." In a slightly more recent report, Glenn (1967, p. 176) tempered this conclusion by muting the stress on the divergence of attitudes by region, but he continued to hold that "it seems unlikely, in view of the data from this and the earlier study, that regional differences have diminished steeply, as it is widely believed."

Results on the attitudes of political tolerance measured in the 1954 and 1973 studies strongly support Glenn's position that regional differences persist. Whether one examines Tolerance Scale scores (Table 35) or attitudes toward wiretapping suspected Communists'

Table 35. Region of Current Residence and Score on Tolerance Scale, National Cross Section, 1954 and 1973.

| Region | Tolerance Scale Scores: | | | |
	Percent Less Tolerant	Percent In-Between	Percent More Tolerant	Number
1954				
West	14	38	48	659
East	15	46	39	1,262
Midwest	16	53	31	1,466
South	29	55	16	1,546
				4,933
1973				
West	8	21	71	609
East	10	25	65	831
Midwest	14	32	54	957
South	25	35	40	1,149
				3,546

telephones (Table 36), the trend of results is toward continued disparities between regions in 1973, as in 1954. Certainly there is no evidence here that public opinion in the four broad regions is becoming homogeneous with respect to political tolerance.

A sharper focus on the changes in political tolerance taking place from 1954 to 1973 is afforded by comparing each region with each other region in expressions of politically tolerant views. As

Table 36. Region of Current Residence and Disposition to Oppose Listening In on Conversations of Suspected Communists, 1954 and 1973.

| | Percent Answering: | | |
| | Should | Should Not | |
Region	Listen In	Listen In	Number
1954			
West	68	32	600
East	67	33	1,153
Midwest	71	29	1,375
South	75	25	1,381
			4,509
1973			
West	37	63	579
East	43	57	796
Midwest	48	52	911
South	57	43	1,076
			3,362

shown in Table 37, from 1954 to 1973 the South dropped further behind the three other regions in four of six comparisons; the Midwest, while maintaining or increasing its distance from the South, likewise declined in political tolerance relative to the East and West; both the East and the West, while remaining similar to one another in

Table 37. Percentage Points by Which Persons Living in Given Regions Lag Behind Persons Living in Other Regions in Expressing Politically Tolerant Responses, 1954 and 1973.

| | Percentage-Point Differences on: | | | |
| | Tolerance Scale | | Listening In on Communists | |
Regions Compared:	1954	1973	1954	1973
South less tolerant than Midwest	15	14	4	9
South less tolerant than East	23	25	8	14
South less tolerant than West	32	31	7	20
Midwest less tolerant than East	8	11	4	5
Midwest less tolerant than West	17	17	3	11
East less tolerant than West	9	6	—[a]	6

[a]In 1954, persons in the East exceeded persons in the West by 1 percentage point in expressing the tolerant response on this measure.

expression of politically tolerant views, generally widened the gap between themselves and the other two regions.

Can the regional differences in political tolerance be interpreted as reflecting cultural variations by region, as being rooted in somewhat distinct versions of the "American way of life"? The information at hand—from this study and from the work of other scholars —is sufficient to raise this issue, but it is inadequate for providing any but the most tentative of answers, except in the case of the South. Beyond the South, we shall need far more research, both historical and contemporary, focused on local and regional populations to approach a definitive understanding of the matter. But it is quite interesting that a serious question regarding the possibility of a regional cultural interpretation arises at all at this time, and it is therefore necessary to sketch the beginnings of a serious answer.

In the South the historical record, humanistic as well as sociological, documents the existence and nature of a regional culture standing alongside the national culture. Reed (1972, p. 83) quite recently assembled convincing evidence of the continuing cultural distinctiveness of the South: "Southerners, we have seen, are more likely than non-Southerners to be conventionally religious, to accept the private use of force (or the potential for it), and to be anchored in their home place. Although the differences are usually in the same direction as the joint effects of the demographic correlates of Southern-ness, they are too large to be ascribed to these correlates. In the American context, and in these respects, in other words, the effect of being Southern is to appear more rural, less educated, and less middle class than one is (or, by Southern standards, the effect of not being Southern is to appear more urban, more educated, and more white collar than one is)."

Localism, defined as a marked preference for and identity with the locale of one's birth, is joined in the South with an insularity of mind that is slow to change, actively belligerent toward the new, and openly intolerant toward a diversity of viewpoints. Hackney (1969, p. 924), in seeking the sources of Southern violence, pointed to a "world view that defines the social, political, and physical environment as hostile and casts the white Southerner in the role of the passive victim of malevolent forces." Although admitting the importance of the historical southern experiences of defeat, frustration, guilt, and poverty which set Southerners apart from other Americans (Woodward, 1968), Hackney (1969, p. 924) suggested that "perhaps they [do] not loom so large as the sense of grievance that is the heart of the Southern identity."*

Given the historically acquired cultural differences just described, the continuing and growing disparity in political toler-ance between the South and other regions is reasonably viewed as arising in part from enduring cultural roots. The contribution of cul-tural background is better revealed by examining the regional responses on one political tolerance measure when the effects of one other important source of political tolerance are controlled. For example, Tables 38 and 39 display Tolerance Scale scores by region controlling for age and education, respectively. Thus, in Table 38 one sees that persons in their twenties and younger in the South are only about as politically tolerant as persons in their forties and fifties out-side the South; in no age grouping do Southerners approximate the Tolerance Scale scores of persons from other regions. Controlling for education level (Table 39) yields similar results. Among the college educated and the grade school educated, the Tolerance Scale scores of Southerners approach, but do not reach, those of Midwesterners; for all other comparisons, persons from the South lag far behind persons from the other regions.†

Yet another way of viewing the cultural distinctiveness of the South in comparison with the other regions is to examine Tolerance Scale scores in relation to stability of region of residence. From this perspective, Table 40 shows that even though persons who have always resided in the West are more tolerant than migrants to the West and persons who have always lived in the East or Midwest are virtually identical in tolerance with migrants to their areas, persons who have always lived in the South are considerably *less* tolerant than are migrants to the South. At the same time, the migrants to the South

*It may be noted that national sample survey data on violence col-lected after Hackney's study reveal the continuing large differences between Southern men and those from other regions in attitudes supportive of vio-lence (Blumenthal, Kahn, Andrews, and Head, 1972, pp. 190–191).

†Williams, Nunn, and St. Peter's (1976a) multivariate analysis also found that regional differences in political tolerance remained after simulta-neously controlling a number of other variables.

Table 38. Age, Current Region of Residence, and Score on Tolerance Scale, 1973.

		Tolerance Scale Scores:			
Age	Region	Percent Less Tolerant	Percent In-Between	Percent More Tolerant	Number
Below 21	West	0	15	85	41
	East	2	27	71	41
	Midwest	0	25	75	44
	South	15	27	58	73
21 to 29	West	2	13	85	142
	East	3	13	84	150
	Midwest	2	20	78	201
	South	11	25	64	247
30 to 39	West	2	20	78	117
	East	8	19	73	155
	Midwest	9	26	65	180
	South	14	34	52	208
40 to 49	West	9	16	74	86
	East	7	28	65	156
	Midwest	10	31	58	156
	South	26	37	37	193
50 to 59	West	8	28	64	94
	East	13	28	59	149
	Midwest	20	37	43	146
	South	27	45	28	163
60 and over	West	18	31	50	119
	East	20	37	43	169
	Midwest	30	44	26	225
	South	50	38	12	242
					3,497

are the least tolerant among all groups of migrants, the migrants to the West and East are the most tolerant, and the migrants to the Midwest occupy a middle position between the South and the other two regions. These distinctive patterns suggest that *each* of the four regions may be attracting somewhat different sorts of persons as well as rearing somewhat different sorts of persons.

The possibility of regional cultural differences gains substance when the migration patterns both between and within the regions are considered. By rearranging the data given in the preceding table, between-region migration patterns can be seen to be greatest in

Table 39. Level of Education, Current Region of Residence, and Score on Tolerance Scale, 1973.

		Tolerance Scale Scores:			
Education	Region	Percent Less Tolerant	Percent In-Between	Percent More Tolerant	Number
College	West	3	8	89	97
graduate	East	2	8	90	158
	Midwest	3	14	83	145
	South	6	16	78	159
Some college	West	3	13	84	166
	East	7	13	80	128
	Midwest	7	18	74	149
	South	9	28	63	176
High school	West	7	28	65	185
	East	8	27	65	282
	Midwest	9	32	59	335
	South	22	31	47	297
Some high	West	12	26	62	82
school	East	17	34	49	149
	Midwest	16	43	41	162
	South	27	46	27	231
Grade school	West	20	34	46	68
	East	20	45	35	105
	Midwest	38	49	13	150
	South	47	44	9	275
					3,499

Table 40. Stability of Region of Residence and Score on Tolerance Scale, 1973.

		Tolerance Scale Score:			
Region of Residence: At Age 16	Current	Percent Less Tolerant	Percent In-Between	Percent More Tolerant	Number
West	West	6	20	74	398
Other	West	11	22	67	211
East	East	10	25	65	711
Other	East	10	24	66	120
Midwest	Midwest	14	31	55	798
Other	Midwest	10	36	54	159
South	South	26	36	38	878
Other	South	21	30	49	271
					3,546

**Table 41. Stability of Region of Residence Between
Age 16 and Adulthood, 1973.**

Current Region of Residence	Percent Stable	Percent In-Migrant	Number
West	65	35	609
South	76	24	1,149
Midwest	83	17	957
East	86	14	831
			3,546

the West and in the South (Table 41). Regarding within-region migration, Hamilton (1965, p. 63), using census data, showed that "the ratio of within-region migration to total population is higher in the South than in the Northeast and North Central [corresponding to the East and Midwest in our usage], but somewhat lower than in the West." Thus, the greatest migration rates both between and within regions occur in the West and South, the very regions that are starkly *dissimilar* with respect to political tolerance. Such an unusual outcome favors the possibility that regional cultural differences exist, and it diminishes the likelihood that the regional differences arise primarily through differences in the heterogeneity of their populations. When placed alongside the persisting regional differences shown to obtain among persons otherwise similar with respect to such basic characteristics as education level, age, and size of place of residence, the idea that regional differences in political tolerance arise in some important part from regional differences in culture becomes deserving of the most careful further study.*

Summary of Findings

We found Americans living in places of larger size to be more politically tolerant than those living in smaller places both in 1954 and in 1973. The differences in democratic restraint associated with size of place of residence are greater in 1973 than they were in 1954.

*Middleton's (1976) recent national study showing antiblack prejudice to be greater in the South than in the non-South is an important beginning. Middleton interpreted the differences as arising from subcultural bases, just as is suggested here.

Much of the explanation for the increasing disparity between urban and rural persons in attitudes of democratic restraint is found in characteristics of individual inhabitants, such as the relatively greater educational levels of city persons in comparison with those of persons living in smaller places; but a portion of the explanation is also found in the heterogeneity and variety afforded by the city.

Regional differences in political tolerance have continued and even increased since 1954. Although the South and Midwest are characterized by lower educational levels and higher proportions of persons living in small towns and on farms than are the West and East, a series of analyses suggests that regional differences in political tolerance may be cultural as well as demographic in origin. The civil libertarian may take heart in the increases in tolerance that occurred in all regions of the country during the period 1954 to 1973; yet the wide and rising disparities in political tolerance existing between the regions in 1973 require careful study. If regional cultural differences are real, and if Americans are selectively migrating in part in recognition of these cultural variations, then future levels of democratic restraint in America will be even more divergent by region than at present. Although diversity in outlook and attitude is usually a democratic virtue and political tolerance is itself a product of diversity, we would much prefer convergence of the regions toward the tolerant consensus.

Chapter 7

Political Tolerance Among Men and Women

/\

If we were to limit ourselves to determining the contributions of various factors to some summary measure of political tolerance, we would not pause long with differences arising from sex. The contribution of sex to score on the Tolerance Scale is negligible, whether in comparison with the import of the variables already considered or viewed solely in its own right (Williams, Nunn, and St. Peter, 1976a). In matters concerning men and women, however, everyone knows that it is especially the subtle nuance that may portend grave and immense outcomes. So it is in the case of men, women, and political tolerance. In view of the vaulting concern for equality between the sexes that has marked the period between the two studies, moreover, the mere persistence of attitudinal differences respecting political tolerance between men and women is remarkable, not to speak of increases in such differences. Much can be learned about contemporary American life by trying to understand the seemingly minor differences in expressing politically tolerant attitudes that persist among men and women.

111

Differences in Tolerance, 1954 and 1973

The most puzzling set of findings in the 1954 study was the thin but persistent edge that men held over women in tolerance. Even when comparisons were made between only those persons equal in educational level, similar in age, sharing the same occupation, participating alike in religious organizations, residing in the same region of the country, or living in places of a particular size, men were found always to give the more tolerant responses in somewhat greater proportions than women.

These results were puzzling not only because no compelling, or even mildly satisfying, explanation could be found for them but also because they confounded accepted notions regarding the characters of American men and women. Certainly in 1954 there was no body of evidence or belief, whether scientific or humanistic, from which to expect greater tolerance among American men than among American women. On the contrary, men were considered more contentious, more striving, more interested in power and especially in exercising power, whereas women were considered more nurturant, more cooperative, more interested in helping others and in preserving others from hurt (Mead, 1949; Ferguson, 1966). Why then were men more tolerant than women of the rights of others? There were no answers.

Differences in tolerance between men and women continue in the 1973 restudy, with one change: the differences are larger in 1973 than they were in 1954. As can be seen in Table 42, in 1954 men held a 7 percentage-point edge over women in the proportion more tolerant; but in 1973, this edge has grown to 16 percentage points. Both men and women have recorded steep gains in tolerance over the time period between the two studies, but men have increased more than women. Table 43 similarly reveals men to have become slightly more tolerant than women with regard to the wiretapping of suspected Communists. In Table 44, summary scores for responses to seven civil liberties questions asked in the 1973 study again disclose men to be more tolerant than women. The 1973 results thus not only repeat the puzzle of men being more tolerant than women; there is now the further riddle that this difference, durable through nearly two decades, has become sturdier.

Table 42. Sex of Respondent and Score on Tolerance Scale, National Cross Section, 1954 and 1973.

Sex of Respondent	Tolerance Scale Scores:			
	Percent Less Tolerant	*Percent In-Between*	*Percent More Tolerant*	*Number*
1954				
Male	17	48	34	2,300
Female	22	51	27	2,632
				4,932
1973				
Male	11	25	64	1,553
Female	19	32	48	1,979
				3,532

Table 43. Sex of Respondent and Disposition to Oppose Listening In on Conversations of Suspected Communists, 1954 and 1973.

Sex of Respondent	Percent Answering:		
	Should Listen In	*Should Not Listen In*	*Number*
1954			
Male	71	29	2,143
Female	71	29	2,365
			4,508
1973			
Male	45	55	1,480
Female	50	50	1,872
			3,352

Table 44. Sex of Respondent and Expression of Politically Tolerant Responses to Seven Questions About Civil Liberties, 1973.

Sex of Respondent	Percent Giving Politically Tolerant Response to:		
	None to Three Questions	*Four to Seven Questions*	*Number*
Male	56	44	1,538
Female	63	37	1,996
			3,534

Some readers may consider the differences between men and women too slight for meaningful analysis. In discussing problems of validity in survey research studies, Phillips (1971, p. 40) cautioned especially against concluding that male-female differences are real without first exploring the possibility that "social desirability response patterns" may account for the differences: "We reasoned that women would be likelier than men to *report* or *admit* to the kinds of acts, behaviors, and feelings that lead to their being categorized as mentally ill, *not* because women actually experienced them more often but rather because it is more culturally appropriate and acceptable in American society for women to be expressive about their difficulties. In other words, it was argued that these symptoms are less socially undesirable for women than for men and that, therefore, women should be more frank about them." But in this light, it seems clear that in both studies it would have been more culturally appropriate and acceptable for men rather than women to express *intolerant* attitudes. The apparently slim differences between men and women take on more substance when viewed, as they properly should be viewed, as reversals of expected trends. Finding in both time periods that men express more tolerant attitudes than women also dismisses any notion that "socially desirable response-sets" are a basis for the male-female differences we report. In any case, recent evidence indicates that "response-style" factors probably are unimportant sources of variance in attitude studies (Bonarius, 1975).

The mystery of differences between men and women in expressions of democratic restraint can be appreciated best by examining levels of tolerance among men and women who share similar characteristics.* To begin with level of education (Table 45), at each level of education men are substantially higher in the proportions more tolerant than women. By far the most intriguing finding is that the greatest difference between men and women, in both time periods, occurs

---

*For expository purposes, our discussion deals only with percentage-point differences between men and women when each of three variables—education level, occupation group, and age—is controlled. The reader is advised that differences between men and women hold also under controls for all other relevant variables for which there are data as well as for all multivariate analyses it would be possible and theoretically relevant to undertake. Men are more politically tolerant than women, under all conditions subject to test by the data.

Table 45. Sex of Respondent, Educational Level, and a Score of More Tolerant on the Tolerance Scale, National Cross Section, 1954 and 1973.

Level of Education	Percent Men	Number	Percent Women	Number
1954				
College graduates	74	193	56	183
Some college	62	199	46	261
High school graduates	46	495	35	712
Some high school	32	465	22	557
Grade school	16	936	12	906
		2,288		2,619
1973				
College graduates	92	323	74	233
Some college	81	291	69	327
High school graduates	66	398	54	697
Some high school	45	262	37	361
Grade school	25	248	14	348
		1,522		1,966

among persons with the *most* education; in both 1954 and 1973, men who are college graduates exceed women who are college graduates in the proportions more tolerant by 18 percentage points—very substantial margins indeed.

Throughout much of the book, it has been argued that increasing levels of education among Americans underlie marked increases in democratic restraint, and of course these data do not bear against the argument. What these results do point to is the greater impact of education among men than among women in affecting levels of political tolerance.

From the standpoint of Borhek's (1965) theory of tolerance, a powerful inequality among men and women arises in work-life experience. Practically all men work outside the home and thus are more likely than women to be exposed to the sorts of diversity that enhance tolerance in the course of their daily lives. Accordingly, if men in particular occupation groups are compared both with women working full time in those occupation groups and with housewives whose husbands are employed in the same occupation groups, then diversity of experience outside the home should be found to produce comparably higher levels of tolerance among the working men and women, while

Table 46. Sex of Respondent, Occupation Group, and a Score of More Tolerant on the Tolerance Scale, 1954 and 1973.

Occupation	Percent Men	Number	Percent Working Women	Number	Percent Housewives	Number
1954						
White collar	53	701	40	409	41	545
Professional	66	180	48	127	50	151
Managerial	49	279	33	76	41	222
Clerical	48	242	37	206	33	172
Blue collar	29	1,033	17	283	23	672
Skilled	37	433	—	—	27	299
Semiskilled	24	340	15	123	21	268
Service	29	105	18	131	21	75
Unskilled	17	155	—	—	19	120
Farm	18	282	23	26	13	254
1973						
White collar	83	659	64	539	62	391
Professional	91	342	73	190	70	80
Managerial	74	177	55	58	—	—
Clerical	73	140	61	291	60	305
Blue collar	55	550	40	294	36	290
Skilled	59	239	—	—	—	—
Semiskilled	52	205	37	130	34	139
Service	60	52	48	108	44	100
Unskilled	43	54	25	36	29	42
Farm	49	45	—	—	—	—

Note: Persons retired at time of interview are excluded from this table. Women reporting a full-time job outside the home, whether married or not, are classified as "working women." All other married women are classified as "housewives" and coded under their husband's occupation. Data for cells with fewer than 25 cases are not shown.

the housewives should display sharply lower levels of tolerance.

But once again, as indicated by the data presented in Table 46, men are distinctly more tolerant than women. Focusing for convenience on the 1973 comparisons (the 1954 data show the same patterns), we find that: among persons in white collar occupations, 83 percent of the men are classified as more tolerant, compared to only 64 percent of the working women and 62 percent of the housewives; in blue collar occupations, 55 percent of the men are classified as more tolerant, compared to only 40 percent of the working women and 36 percent of the housewives. Comparing other occupation groups on the table would disclose the same pattern: among persons in comparable statuses, men are markedly more tolerant than women. Counter to theory, the experience of working outside the home does not affect the tolerance levels of women at all.

The pervasiveness of the differences in tolerance between men and women may be demonstrated further by observing results for persons of various ages. The data in Table 47 affirm that men express

Table 47. Sex of Respondent, Age, and a Score of
More Tolerant on the Tolerance Scale, 1954 and 1973.

Age	Percent Men	Number	Percent Women	Number
1954				
21 to 29	48	384	37	520
30 to 39	42	534	33	640
40 to 49	35	534	28	524
50 to 59	29	378	23	416
60 and above	19	467	14	531
1973				
21 to 29	79	341	73	397
30 to 39	72	303	59	357
40 to 49	64	277	48	314
50 to 59	60	228	37	324
60 and above	37	287	24	468

more democratic restraint than women across the entire life span and for both time periods studied. Further scrutiny of this table discloses one small surprise that leads at last to fresh understanding. Comparing the 1954 and 1973 data, one finds that the differences in tolerance between men and women are greater in 1973 than in 1954 for all age groups except the youngest. Among persons in their twenties, the male advantage in tolerance has been pared from 11 percentage points in 1954 to 6 percentage points in 1973. This apparently slim bit of evidence of a reversal in the otherwise clear trend toward a widening gap in levels of tolerance between men and women provides the clue to fathoming the mystery of sex differences in political tolerance being tracked in this chapter.

Why should women in their twenties in 1973 begin to approach the Tolerance Scale scores of their male agemates, while the scores of women in all other age groupings continue to fall further behind those of men? These divergent trends make a great deal of intuitive sense when one recalls that persons in their twenties in 1973 have experienced during their young lives only the post–World War II social climate, with its many features supporting equality between the sexes. The oldest persons in this age cohort were just nineteen years old in 1963 when Friedan's *The Feminine Mystique*, destined to symbolize the changing relations between the sexes in our culture, was published. Far more than any previous generation of Americans, these young men and women have shared a common culture. During the short span of their lives, federal and state laws protecting better than ever before the rights of women have proliferated. This is no doubt the first generation of Americans among whom large numbers of both sexes have agreed that women should enjoy the same range of choices as men, whether in career, sexual activity, or any other human endeavor.*

Now the point of all this argument is not that equality between the sexes in any sphere of American life has emerged in the recent past but that over the past twenty-five years a surge of equalitarian activity unprecedented in scope has taken place in American life and that this activity has culminated in young women experiencing, by and large, the diversity of the world around them in nearly the same fullness as do young men. Unencumbered by the customary expectations binding their older sisters to home, children, and family concerns, these young women confront the larger worlds outside marriage—the worlds of work, politics, ideas. This new openness to the

---

*Among persons with similar educational levels, women typically lead men in endorsing new ways of expressing equality between the sexes, and the young always lead older people in this matter (Bernard, 1974).

sweep and complexity of the larger world, then, gives rise to tolerant attitudes among young women to nearly the levels found among young men.

Apart from the merit of this line of speculation in explaining the recent move toward convergence among young men and women in levels of tolerance, the discussion brings forward at last the most probable basis for the continuing divergence in tolerant attitudes of the main bulk of American men and women. The mysterious male advantage in attitudes of democratic restraint may be understood as a lingering consequence of inequality between the sexes in American society. The concept of inequality between the sexes comprehends, of course, a set of social conditions that are changing, and which in changing affect Americans of different ages differently. Such a concept possesses the scope and power to suggest why men are more tolerant politically than women even when they share such indicators of diverse experience as the same level of education and type of occupation, the same place of residence, and the same degree of participation in organized community life. Representing all the ways in which American men have enjoyed dominion, privilege, responsibility, and diversity both of expectations and of experiences in comparison with. women, the concept rationalizes the mystery of men being more politically tolerant than women.

Although this account of the perplexing differences in democratic restraint between men and women cannot be tested adequately at the present time, the passage of years should permit definitive tests. If inequality between the sexes in the United States declines, so also should differences in political tolerance between men and women; if inequalities based on sex become more pronounced, then the differences in tolerance between men and women should mount. Whatever the future course of events, the small yet steady trend over the past two decades toward more political tolerance among men than among women bears silent witness to the continuing inequality between the sexes in the United States.

Summary of Findings

In both 1954 and 1973, men express politically tolerant attitudes somewhat more frequently than do women. Comparing men and women who share similar levels of education, types of occupation, and age, the 1954 and 1973 data reveal an increasing disparity in political tolerance of men and women *except for the youngest persons.* We suggest that inequality between the sexes restricts the diversity of experience for women in comparison with men, resulting in lower political tolerance among women than among men. If equality between the sexes becomes manifest throughout our society, differences in political tolerance between men and women should disappear. Concern over the morality of differences in opportunities between the sexes, that is, concern over the wrongness of the double standard and the rightness of equality between the sexes, may be sufficient to *involve* young adults in new ways of thinking and behaving; over the span of a lifetime, however, many changes in the institutions of the family, school, and work place would be required to *sustain* persons in these ideas and activities. Signs of such basic institutional change are not especially prominent today.* Continued variation or a new convergence in levels of political tolerance between men and women depends on whether life opportunities for women continue to be blocked or equality is allowed to emerge.

*If contemporary adolescent experiences at home, in school, and among peers forecast accurately the contours of adult personality, then the picture presented by Douvan and Gold (1966) in their inclusive review of research on adolescence holds no promise of basic change in American male and female characters. Reviewing research on women's achievement in work in the late 1960s, Rosen, Crockett, and Nunn (1969) concluded that prospects for female equality in the world of work were remote. The most recent assessment of women's achievements in science details the continuing inequality of women's participation in science (Zuckerman and Cole, 1975). The absence of fundamental change in the schools has been charted by many authors; Frazier and Sadker (1973) provide a recent account.

Chapter 8

Religion and
Individual Freedom

/\

The roots of this country are solidly fixed in the pursuit of freedom of conscience. The first article of the Bill of Rights leaves no doubt about the importance of religious freedom and freedom of conscience in general: "Congress shall make no law respecting an establishment of religion, or prohibiting the free exercise thereof; or abridging the freedom of speech, or of the press; or the right of the people peaceably to assemble and to petition the Government for a redress of grievances." Indeed, this article of the Bill of Rights explicitly links religious freedom with civil liberties of speech, press, assembly, and petition.

As with other freedoms, actual accomplishment of religious freedom has been neither automatic nor inevitable. Long and difficult struggles for freedom of conscience dot American history. Nor has the seemingly logical interdependence of individual freedom to believe according to conscience, to speak one's mind, to print without censorship, and to peaceably voice grievances been unambiguously recognized in the Great American Experiment.

Most information social science has to offer on the relationship of religiosity and tolerant attitudes toward those who are different gives us little reason to conclude that those who are religious, who might be expected to value individual liberty of conscience, are the vanguards of tolerance toward variety in society. On the contrary, Americans who are most committed to religious institutions are typically among the most ethnocentric—the least willing to extend the benefit of the doubt.

Although research on religion and support of civil liberties has been sparse, the related issue of religion and prejudice has been copiously researched. The results are not always consistent, but an overall appraisal of the evidence indicates that when the religious are defined as those who value and participate in organized religion, they are most often counted among the prejudiced of the society. But this conclusion is too simple to explain the complex relationship between religiosity and attitudes toward people who are different. Recent research demonstrates that the issue is confounded by the interplay of social, psychological, cultural, and religious factors. Even the conception of what is religious has been changing among scientists, serving both to expand our understanding and reveal the relationship of religion and racial attitude as a complex one.

Dittes (1969) put together one of the most thoughtful and thorough syntheses of research on this issue. If we consider the most general, and probably the least profitable, approach to religiosity, major faith affiliation, the research evidence is neither clear nor consistent. Where differences were found, Jews were least prejudiced, Protestants next, and Catholics most prejudiced. Others, however, have found no differences between major faiths (Dittes, 1969, p. 635). Lenski (1963) found that Jews, Protestants, and Catholics, in that order, supported free speech. Among college students, Nunn (1973) reported Catholics to be more supportive than Protestants of the principles of the Bill of Rights, especially among active religious participants.

Surely level of religious participation is a more meaningful sociological variable than faith affiliation, particularly since we know that denominational differences among Protestants in such attitudes as libertarianism are often greater than Protestant-Catholic differences (Glock and Stark, 1966). This assumption is supported by the growing body of evidence indicating that when the full range of religious attendance, from no attendance to frequent attendance, is considered, a provocative curvilinear pattern often emerges between attendance and conservative attitudes like racial and ethnic prejudice (Dittes, 1969, p. 630). That is, the least prejudiced are more likely to be either highly active or totally inactive attenders, and the most prejudiced are most often the moderate attenders.

Such a pattern has stimulated a number of researchers to think about new interpretations of religiosity. The search for new interpretations has gone in several directions, but all in the pursuit of what can be called styles of religiousness. Wilson (1960) and Allport and Ross (1967), for example, attempted to find a distinction between "intrinsic" and "extrinsic" religiousness, between those who have personal and devout styles of religiosity (intrinsic) and those who tend to pursue religion for more utilitarian reasons (extrinsic). Stark and Glock (1969), in one of the most influential attempts to expand conceptualizations and measurements of religiosity, specified five different dimensions of religiosity: ideological (beliefs), ritualistic (religious practice), experiential (feelings), intellectual (knowledge), and consequential (effects on conduct).* But the best single indicator of religious commitment, according to Stark and Glock (1968), is an index of religious beliefs.

When Stark and Glock (1968, p. 93) compared responses to their measure of religious beliefs (the Orthodoxy Index) with measures of religious libertarianism (extending civil liberties to atheists), they found a strong propensity for those who were highly libertarian to be low on religious orthodoxy. But their claim that anti-Semitism is predictable from levels of orthodoxy of beliefs was questioned by Dittes (1969), who pointed out that they changed the nature of their index by overloading it with anti-Jewish items. Other recent research on religiosity and social attitudes also discounts the causative power of religious beliefs. Aiming primarily at the Glock-Stark argument that Christian beliefs have sizable and direct effects on anti-Semitism, Middleton (1973) and Hoge and Carroll (1975) presented evidence of personality determinants of anti-Semitism. Ploch (1974), in a reanal-

---

*Others have tested and elaborated on these efforts so that we can now speak of religiousness as involving a variety of styles and dimensions which are intercorrelated to some extent but which have considerable independence of content as well. James Dittes (1969) provides an excellent review of the research on this issue.

ysis of the Glock and Stark data, found that socioeconomic variables were more significant than religious beliefs as sources of anti-Semitism. Research by Whitt and Nelsen (1975) also indicated that if one assumes moral traditionalism (for example, prohibition of drinking and gambling) is not a part of conservative theology, social factors (especially education) have a significant impact on levels of tolerance of atheists. A variety of other studies, however, consistently show a correlation between doctrinal orthodoxy and ethnocentric attitudes (Dittes, 1969).

Strommen's (Strommen and others, 1972) research is a noteworthy exception to most findings on the relation of orthodoxy to social attitudes. He and his associates found that religious conservatism was unrelated to conservative social attitudes. It is important to remember, as Dittes (1969) reminded us, that Strommen's sample was relatively homogeneous and clustered at the upper levels of orthodoxy.

To view religiosity as complex and multidimensional is clearly a step forward, but it involves new problems. One such problem derives from recent measures of religious beliefs. Others have criticized the Glock-Stark study for the contamination of their religious beliefs measure with items that have no direct relevance to religious belief (Dittes, 1969; Hoge and Carroll, 1973, 1975; Spilka, 1971). It might also be argued that the Glock-Stark orthodoxy index fundamentally taps cognitive rigidity within the broad domain of religious literalism. Thus, it is not surprising that orthodoxy indices and nonreligious measures of dogmatism, intolerance of ambiguity, and the like are usually closely correlated. Rokeach (1960) alerted us to the importance of distinguishing styles and intensity of beliefs from their content, but most of the research has concentrated on the intensity of belief rather than on content (Strommen and others, 1972). This is not to say that understanding the relationship of religious and nonreligious belief rigidity is unimportant, but, as others have noted, the symbolic nature of religious beliefs instructs us to look at belief as a symbolic process that often incorporates ambivalent elements. Paul W. Pruyser (1974) has appropriately extended this concern to include unbelief as well as belief.

If religious beliefs are to be taken seriously, and both traditional and contemporary evidence implores us to do so, then the intensity and symbolic content of beliefs become proper areas of concern for those trying to understand the persistence of religious beliefs, particularly in the modern pluralistic society. The extent to which the development and function of religious beliefs can be understood depends in large measure not only on taking beliefs seriously but on searching for the linkages between beliefs, personality, and sociocultural forces. True, it is important to know the relative predictive power and causal sequence of these components, but it is also important to understand why and under what conditions religious beliefs correlate with nonreligious phenomena. Approaches that focus on the isolation of religious and nonreligious effects often assume sharp distinctions of the sacred and secular and even of personality and social components, and in so doing obscure the subtleties of interrelationships.

Whatever else religion is, it is defined here as a cultural institution functioning in various social contexts, selectively attracting individuals with particular needs and directly or indirectly affecting their attitudes and behavior. Acute dichotomies between the sacred and secular muddy the interesting issues inherent in religion-society-personality relationships. Much of the debate about the impact of secularization on religion, for example, fails to give due attention to intriguing questions about the persistence of traditional religious forms, new religious consciousness, the adaptability of religion to social change—in short, about religion's dynamic qualities.

Few would deny that secular forces have had a powerful effect on religion. Some celebrate the effect (Cox, 1966; Berger, 1961). Others, especially conservative forces in religion, view the impact of modernity with contempt and retrench to protect the purity and sacredness of religion (Greeley, 1972). Most social scientists would agree that the weight of the evidence reveals the dominant thrust of religion to be a conserving and legitimizing force, hence resistant to secularizing forces. While this position may be an accurate reflection of empirical reality, it has distracted us from important issues, some of which were noted above. It also runs the risk of considering conservative religion as nonsecularized, thus directing attention from the possibility that conservative religion might also be secularized but in different ways from liberal religion.

The problem rests on distinctions and definitions of the sacred and secular. The central focus of secularizing effects on religion has been on social attitudes and actions. During the 1960s, when several events exacerbated internal conflict in the general society and religion in particular (Hadden, 1969), social action became the catchword for the secularization debate. If liberal social attitudes and actions are accepted as the crux of the secularization issue, then a good case can be made for the distinction between worldly secularism and other-worldly sacredness. However, if one accepts that all religious groups and individuals operate within the confines of a sociocultural context and that religion contributes to the interpretation and meaning of that context and one's place in it, then the question becomes *how* and *why* religious groups or individuals are connected to the secular order, not merely whether one religious group or style is more secularized than another, or even whether or not religion has become secularized.

Throughout history, church and state have been more or less intimately intertwined. Earlier, the mix tended to be explicit. In recent times, as the power of the political establishment has become more pronounced, the relationship of religion and politics has become more subtle, taking the form of "civil religion," as Bellah (1967) described it. The election of Southern Baptist Jimmy Carter as President will not reinstate the explicit link between religion and state, but it is a vivid reminder of the subtle nature of the relationship.

The evidence of social science points to a strong and abiding correlation of religion and politics (Lipset, 1964). Religion, ethnicity, and social class are also closely fettered (Demerath, 1965; Lazerwitz, 1964). Even when it appears that a religious group is detached and otherworldly (typically lower-class and working-class congregations), there are usually subtle but clear indications of in-the-world relevance in the religious style (Johnson, 1961). Other research shows close ties between religion and secular variables, but the point here is that most religious groups function in a secular order that requires some accommodation to that secular world. The critical question then is not just which religious groups are more accommodated than others, but how is accommodation made, and what implications does it have for the style of religiosity displayed and sociopolitical attitudes expressed?

This chapter will attempt to understand the complex relationship between religious beliefs and social and personality factors, and in turn the consequence of their interrelationships for political tolerance. But first we shall consider the larger picture of how religiosity has changed in America.

Religious Affiliation, 1954 to 1973

As our discussion thus far makes clear, much of the debate about the rise, decline, or changing nature of religion is grounded in conceptual and measurement problems. Just exactly what religion and religiosity are will continue to be a major concern of social scientists, even though considerable progress has been made in the past decade. It now seems evident, however, that religiosity has several dimensions.

If we take the crudest indicators of religiousness available, religious affiliation and attendance, we find that only moderate shifts have taken place among rank-and-file Americans between 1954 and 1973. By these indicators most Americans claim some religious identification, and a majority attend religious services with some regularity. The comparison of affiliations in 1954 and 1973 shows only a moderate decline in the proportion Protestant, from 73 percent in 1954 to 64 percent in 1973. The proportion of adults who are Catholics, Jews, or some other religion has changed very little. In 1954, 21 percent of the sample were Catholic, 3 percent were Jewish, and 1 percent claimed some other affiliation. In 1973, 23 percent were Catholic, 4 percent were Jewish, and 3 percent were affiliated with another religion. Nor does there appear to have been a wave of defections from some religious identification to none. The proportion claiming no affiliation increased only slightly, from 2 percent in 1954 to 6 percent in 1973.

Religious attendance declined only moderately during the nineteen-year period. The Gallup Poll reported a gradual decline in attendance from 1955 to 1974, with 49 percent attending church or synagogue during an average week in 1955 and 40 percent attending in 1974. Much of that decline appears to have been among Catholics, especially in the last decade. In 1954, 63 percent reported that they attended church or synagogue in the month preceding the interview; by 1973, this percentage had dropped to 54 percent.

Community leaders follow a similar but sharper trend than those of the rank and file: all categories but Protestants showed an increase in religious affiliation since 1954. The consequence of this shift is to make the distribution of religions among community leaders more exactly reflect the distribution of religious affiliations among the general populace. At least at the local level, Protestants no longer appear to disproportionately dominate leadership posts as they did in 1954. The reader should be reminded, however, that the community leader samples were drawn from cities with 10,000 to 150,000 populations.

Community leaders also differ from community members in religious participation. Both in 1954 and in 1973, leaders were more active church and synagogue attenders than the general public. Nonetheless, leaders experienced about the same degree of decline in religious service attendance as did the rank and file: in 1954, 77 percent of the local leaders reported attending religious services in the month prior to the interview; in 1973, only 67 percent reported attending.

Religious Affiliation, Participation, and Tolerance for Nonconformity

Organized religion persists as a reasonably active part of the majority of Americans' lives. Do religious Americans, as indicated by religious affiliations and attendance, support the principles of the Bill of Rights by extending civil liberties to those who are not political and religious mainstream Americans?

The answer to the question is straightforward, according to our findings. Those who identify with a particular religious institution, with the exception of Jews, and those who attend religious services are less likely to be tolerant of nonconformists than citizens who claim no affiliation and do not participate in religious services. The differences are usually clear cut.

Consider the findings presented in Table 48, which shows the proportions scoring more tolerant on the Tolerance Scale for different religious affiliates and nonaffiliates. All religious groups are becoming more tolerant of nonconformists, but those who claim no religious affiliation are clearly more tolerant than those who identify

Table 48. Religious Affiliations of the Rank and File and
Community Leaders and a Score of More Tolerant on the
Tolerance Scale, 1954 and 1973.

Religious Affiliation	Percent in 1954	Number	Percent in 1973	Number
Rank and file				
Protestant	28	3,581	46	1,920
Catholic	31	1,047	59	832
Jew	71	158	88	141
Other	46	59	60	396
None	49	88	87	229
Leaders				
Protestant	63	1,198	82	329
Catholic	63	229	77	155
Jew	77	53	94	31
Other	—[a]		—[a]	
None	80	15	100	31

[a] Too few cases for stable percentages.

with a religious group, except for Jewish respondents. This trend holds true for both the general public and the community leader samples in 1973. The most dramatic change was among the nonaffiliates of the rank and file. In 1954, 49 percent of those with no religious affiliation were classified as more tolerant; by 1973, that percentage had swelled to 87 percent.

Differences among religious groups also persist for the general public and local civic leaders, with the latter group functioning as a rough control for the effects of education, since over three fourths of the leaders have had some college training. Protestants were least likely to be tolerant in both the 1954 and the 1973 rank-and-file samples, but Catholics hold that dubious honor among leaders in 1973. Nevertheless, all community leaders are more tolerant than their religious counterparts in the general public.

Another way of locating the significance of organized religion for political attitudes is to determine who were the more active devotees to a particular religion. Like Stouffer in 1954, we asked respondents in the 1973 survey if they had attended church or synagogue in the month preceding the interview. We found that, in each major faith, the people more committed to their religious group—that is, those who attended more frequently—were less tolerant than the religiously less active, both in the 1954 and in the 1973 surveys and in rank-and-file and leader samples. In the general public sample, however, the differences between the attenders and nonattenders were even greater in 1973 than in 1954.

Nevertheless, both the religiously active and the religiously inactive have become more tolerant. In 1954, 35 percent of the rank and file who did not attend church or synagogue were classified as more tolerant; by 1973, this figure had risen to 62 percent. Among the religiously active, 28 percent in 1954 and 48 percent in 1973 scored as more tolerant. However, among community leaders, the religiously active made greater gains (61 percent to 80 percent) than the nonactive (73 percent to 88 percent) in the proportion scoring more tolerant.

When responses from a second question (asked in 1973 but not in 1954) about respondents' typical attendance records are considered, religious service attendance is even more clearly linked to levels of tolerance. Seven frequency categories were presented to the respondents, ranging from attendance more than once a week to never. With each reduction in level of frequency of church and synagogue attendance there was a corresponding reduction of the proportion more tolerant among the general public. Thirty-six percent of the most active attenders were more tolerant, as opposed to 69 percent of those who never attend. The curvilinear relationship between attendance and social attitudes reported by others was not observed in the 1973 survey data.

Religiously active and inactive Americans were also asked specifically if they would be willing to let someone who was against churches and religion speak to their community. Here too, those who attended religious services were less tolerant than those who did not attend. Although the proportion of attenders and nonattenders willing to let an atheist speak increased between 1954 and 1973, nonattenders were becoming more tolerant at a more rapid rate. In 1954, 34 percent of those who attended religious services and 43 percent of those who did not were willing to give atheists freedom of speech. By 1973, these figures had risen to 57 percent for attenders and 69 percent for nonattenders. These results reinforce our initial claim that tolerance as defined here is not just an attitude that easily fluctuates with prevailing self-interests. In 1973 well over a majority with the greatest stake in organized religion were willing to tolerate those most threatening to that interest.

Frequency of attendance and nominal identification with a religious faith certainly cannot be construed as the best indicators of religiosity, but the evidence is consistent and telling. Americans, both rank and file and local leaders, who are "religious" in these ways may view themselves as decent people who are ready to extend constitutional freedoms to their fellow citizens, but the evidence does not confirm their self-image. Instead, they must be counted among the most intolerant of our society.

Religious Beliefs and Tolerance for Nonconformity

However, some would say that religious *beliefs* must be considered as a central measure of religiosity, not the "superficialities" of going or not going to religious services. As discussed above, sociologists, recognizing the validity of this argument, have taken steps to improve on past conceptions of religiosity and its measurement. Unfortunately, the 1954 survey was completed prior to these advancements and did not include questions about religious beliefs; the 1973 survey did. The 1973 survey asked some of the same religious belief questions that Glock and Stark (1966) asked of a national sample in 1964, so comparisons can be made with that study, which was completed at approximately the midpoint between the 1954 study and the 1973 survey. Glock has made the 1964 survey available to us for that purpose, and the findings are surprising: since 1964, the certainty of belief that God exists has declined in the nation, while the certainty that the Devil exists has increased! Table 49 gives the details.

Fewer Americans in 1973 than in 1964 were absolutely certain that God exists, a decline of 8 percent. The Devil, however, appears to be getting his due. By 1973 the percentage of Americans completely sure of the Devil's existence had increased to 50 percent, a change of 13 percent since 1964. Before examining the relationship of tolerance and religion as measured by beliefs, let us consider the implications of these findings.

Does this finding indicate an American fad of Devil worship?*

---

*Much of the discussion that follows is adapted from Nunn (1974).

Table 49. Certainty of Religious Beliefs, 1964 and 1973.

Religious Beliefs	Percent in 1964	Percent in 1973	Percent Change
God exists			
Absolutely certain	77	69	-8
Some doubts	15	19	+4
Higher power but no personal God	5	6	+1
Don't know or don't believe God exists	3	6	+3
Number of respondents	1,970	3,542	
The Devil exists			
Completely true	37	50	+13
Probably true	28	21	-7
Probably not or definitely not true	26	27	+1
Don't know or other	9	2	-7
Number of respondents	1,910	3,408 [a]	

[a]To make 1964 and 1973 samples comparable, 131 Jews were omitted.

The data presented in Table 49, indicating that there has been a decline in God's credibility and a rise in the Devil's, suggests that Satanism is making dramatic gains in America, but detailed analyses indicate something quite different.

Overwhelmingly, those certain about the Devil's existence are God-believing, church-going Christians. The increasing doubt in God's existence thus comes from a portion of the population other than those people firmly believing in the Devil. Ninety-four percent of those completely certain the Devil exists are also absolutely certain that God exists; only one person in the entire sample was certain that the Devil exists but not absolutely sure that God exists.

There are two trends taking place. One, the decline in certainty about God, appears to be the result of the often noted modernizing forces in the society. The second trend, the increasing credibility of the Devil, springs from other sources.

Consistently, we found that the more active the participation in religious services, the greater the likelihood that people were certain that the Devil was around, particularly among Protestants and Catholics in the Bible Belts of America. Among the most active religious attenders (more than once a week), 83 percent believed it was completely true that the Devil exists. As frequency of attendance declined, certainty of the Devil's existence declined.

Why do people believe in the Devil? We may profitably review this question from a sociocultural perspective. Durkheim (1912) makes the connection between the religious (sacred) and the social (profane), between a specific attitude of respect for the sacred and a respectful attitude toward moral obligation and authority. Others (Swanson, 1960) have since elaborated and specified Durkheim's theoretical rationale, but his basic proposition was a major sociological insight.

Societies by definition must maintain a minimal degree of order and a core of meaning that sustains and gives that social order internal legitimacy. The fact that individuals are born into an existing society maintaining an institutional network that continues to ensure the sovereignty of a society gives the society power to command respect and obedience from members. But, Durkheim argues, beliefs that one's society has some ultimate, sacred overlayer play a vital part in legitimizing that social order. Societal members come not only to regard their society as *their* society but ultimately to regard it as having a supremacy that makes it "right," if not absolutely the best of all societies. This tendency is what gives rise to the belief that God is always on the side of one's own society in intersocietal conflict.

The centrality of religion to social order and meaning, of course, wanes with the escalation of industrialization and modernity (Glock and Stark, 1965; Yinger, 1970), but religion has far from disappeared even in modern societies. One needs only to consider again the percentage of Americans in Table 49 who still believe with some certainty in the supernatural to be convinced religiosity is still very much around. However, that religion changes its form and function with the advancement of modernization is also apparent. Berger (1967) adds that the flow of influence between religion and society is more exactly dialectical than unilateral. So it becomes important to ask if religion persists in modern societies in its Durkheimian connection, linking respect for religious authority with social authority, the sacred with the profane.

We approximated the Durkheimian linkage of the sacred and profane from two statements. The first statement was: *"Most of the problems of this world result from the fact that more and more people are moving away from God."* The second statement, corresponding to the first but put in terms of respect for social authority, was: *"One of*

Table 50. The Link Between Sacred and Profane Authority.

Major Prob- lem Is Not Accepting What Lead- ers Tell Us	Most Problems Due to a Move Away from God:					
	Percent Strongly Agree	Percent Agree	Percent Don't Know	Percent Disagree	Percent Strongly Disagree	Number
Strongly agree	64	17	1	13	5	154
Agree	53	28	2	13	4	1,391
Don't know	48	26	12	13	1	211
Disagree	35	34	1	22	8	1,546
Strongly disagree	26	19	1	19	35	234

the major problems in this country is that too many people are unwilling to accept what our leaders try to tell us.'' Table 50 gives the results of the cross tabulation of the two questions. Clearly, those who attributed national maladies to a failure to heed our leaders were, for the most part, also those who saw our problems resulting from a rejection of God.

Of those who agreed with the first statement, 74 percent were also convinced of the existence of the Devil. Only 20 percent of those who strongly rejected this view of world problems were inclined to be certain about the Devil. Similar patterns are found among those who reported a strong sense of threat to our way of life from Communism and revolution; of these, 81 and 76 percent, respectively, were absolutely certain of God. The corresponding figures for those not threatened by these forces were 52 and 64 percent.

We do not suggest that those most committed to the American way of life will necessarily be most devoted to God, nor that those less devoted to God will be less committed to the society. The findings do suggest, however, that the more firmly people believe in God, the more firmly—perhaps blindly—patriotic they are to a traditional social authority and the more sensitive they are to threats to that fixed order. In this sense Durkheim's claim still holds true. But in the modern world other forces forge commitments to the social order that are of a different quality. Greater education, for instance, is likely to lead to rejection of simplified explanations, such as falling away from God, as well as to a reduced sense of threat from disruptive forces. In the 1973 survey sample, 52 percent of those with less than a high school education, but only 28 percent with a high school education or more, strongly agreed that the world's problems were due to a rejection of God. The threat of Communism and revolution produced similar patterns with education. These patterns did not occur because the more educated were less committed to the continuity of society but because their commitment is likely to be of a different quality (Harris, 1973). The more educated have resources to enhance their comprehension and to minimize their dependency on traditional authority. Such resources give the educated ties to social order and authority that are qualitatively different from those of the less educated. Consequently, we can expect not only that the relatively powerless and uneducated will be committed to society in a different manner than more powerful and educated citizens but also that there will be differential responses to failures and discontentments in the society.

If, as our findings suggest, God and one's society are intimately bound together, and God is "good," how is dissatisfaction within society reconciled? Theologically, another power, the Devil, is seen to operate in the world causing evil (incomprehensible, diabolical acts that cause people and societies to degenerate). It is our thesis that belief in the Devil plays an important part both in reducing the tension spawned by the commitment of the powerless and less educated to their society and in lessening their awareness of the failure and discontentment present in the society itself. Thus, the Devil is seen as the source of failure and imperfections in the society; in this way, the institutional question is diverted and some sense of comprehension and social order perceived.

Every failure in the society, of course, is not attributed to the Devil even by believers. The American cultural value of individualism, which cuts across socioeconomic lines, encourages self-blame for personal failures. The religious counterpart of this cultural value is found in the great emphasis, especially among the powerless, on personal sin and demon possession. Hill (1968), for example, has concluded that the pervasive and enduring theme of southern Protestantism is salvation of the individual, not social reconstruction.

Culturally prescribed individualism can go a long way toward alleviating the social tension aggravated by individual failures, but not without social and personal costs. And what happens when the failures are undeniably more pervasive than one's own isolated case?

The more powerful and socially conscious have recourse to

efforts to change the social structure, to replace the leadership, or, in frustration, to retreat into new variations of fundamentalistic religion and to the occult (Berger, Berger, and Kellner, 1974). The limited resources, restricted knowledge, and loyalty to authority can reduce the powerless to chronic frustration and to a belief in the Devil as the author of diabolical events. Even for Devil believers, dissonance may be reduced, but their frustration may resurface in other forms (a point we will return to shortly).

The frustration generated by the powerless and uneducated's situation is well illustrated by John Steinbeck's account in *The Grapes of Wrath* ([1939] 1967, pp. 52–53) of the tenant farmer being forced off his land and out of his home. As a bulldozer approaches his place to plow it under, the farmer rushes out with his shotgun ready to kill the driver. The bulldozer driver quickly explains that the farmer should not shoot him because he was just doing what he was ordered to do. "Who gave you orders? I'll go after him." The driver replies that the farmer's intentions to shoot his boss are wrong because the boss got his orders from the bank, and the bank in turn got orders from "the East" to make the land profitable. In final desperation to find someone to blame and punish, the farmer asks, "But where does it stop? Who can we shoot? I don't aim to starve to death before I kill the man that's starving me." The driver responds, "I don't know. Maybe there's nobody to shoot. Maybe the thing isn't men at all. Maybe, like you said, the property's doing it."

Steinbeck's farmer finally realizes the futility of trying to find a person to blame and kill. It would be easy to believe, in this interpretation, that the farmer's helplessness and ambivalence led him to see the Devil's hand in these events, since the overwhelming hardships he felt were widespread in the Dust Bowl days of the 1930s.

The novelist can orchestrate the outcome of events as he sees fit, but the social researcher must be guided by the dictates of the data. Our theoretical expectations are that when the quality of life is generally viewed as being tipped toward a worsening state of affairs rather than toward the more optimistic side of the balance, especially among those with limited resources to comprehend and affect society, the Devil's credibility should increase. While we did not have a question that asked about the balance of "good" and "evil" in society, we approximated the balance from a question that forced a choice between two alternatives: (1) *"While we have problems now, the world is becoming a better place to live in every day"* or (2) *"The world has more problems now than it has ever had and things are getting worse."* Education was used as the indicator of resources to comprehend and affect outcomes.

While the association of perceived quality of life and certainty of the Devil holds true for both educational levels, it is stronger for the less educated (Gamma = .24) than the better educated (Gamma = .17). When life is believed to be falling apart, the Devil is given greater credibility. Conversely, when life is thought to be improving, the Devil is less believable.

Why has there been a shift in belief in the Devil? While the sociology of religious beliefs has focused almost entirely on belief in God, the popular interest in the Devil and the evidence presented here raise some questions about the Devil's place in the scheme of things and why the Devil's credibility has increased since 1964. Taking the stance that belief in God is intimately linked with a concern for social meaning and order, we have argued that the Devil's credibility is closely tied to the feeling that the institutional order is seriously threatened and that the balance of "good" and "evil" is being tipped toward the latter. Greater certainty about the Devil is most often found among the least educated, who have the greatest dependency on, least input into, and least comprehension of the social order. Instead of being viewed as random, irrational behavior, belief in the Devil is interpreted as an effort by the powerless to make sense of the world, to apply causality when disorder threatens, and to reduce the dissonance generated by their commitment to a societal order that is incomprehensible and unresponsive to them.

To explain the surge in the Devil's credibility in the last decade, according to our interpretation, we need to demonstrate that it was among the less educated and those most religious that belief in the Devil showed the greatest rise. We should also show that there has been an increase in uncertainty about the society or a feeling that things are getting out of control.

Table 51 shows that growth in the percentage certain that the Devil exists was in fact greater among the less educated and among religious adherents than among the more educated and the less religiously active. All categories showed an increase in the percentage

Table 51. Certainty of the Devil by Education and
Religious Attendance, 1964 and 1973.

Education and Religious Attendance	Percent Certain of the Devil: 1964	1973	Percent Change
Education			
Some high school	41	63	+22
High school graduate	44	53	+9
Some college	38	41	+3
College graduate	30	33	+3
Religious attendance			
Once a week or more	50	69	+19
1 to 3 times a month	35	51	+16
Once a year	27	37	+10
Less than once a year	21	30	+9

certain of the Devil, but the greatest increases were found among those who were not high school graduates and those who were more religiously active.

Second, while there was no directly comparable question to indicate changes in perceived quality of life, there were some similar indicators and indirect evidence of a decade of uncertainty and social strain. Indeed, so much occurred in the last decade that it would seem unnecessary to empirically establish the point. The Vietnam War was brought to an end, but the years preceding the disengagement were filled with protests that the war was morally wrong. The late 1960s also saw the peaking of racial protests. One survey reported that 75 percent of our high schools experienced some form of unrest during 1968–69 (Department of Justice, 1969). Assassinations of national leaders in 1968 added to the discontent. All major institutional areas of leadership showed substantial drops in public confidence from 1966 to 1973 (Etzioni and Nunn, 1974). Even science and technology, which in previous decades appeared to hold the promise of an unspoiled progression toward utopia, were increasingly viewed with mixed feelings. And Watergate, of course, contributed its share of uncertainty about the future.

Although the 1973 data were collected before Watergate became an all-consuming crisis, anxieties about it were apparent from the slump in the President's popularity and in the percentage of people who felt "there was something deeply wrong in America today." Harris (1973) reported that in March 1968, 39 percent of the American public felt there was something "deeply wrong," and by 1973 that figure had increased to 48 percent. The feeling was especially acute among the less educated (67 percent). Harris (1973) also reported that powerlessness had almost doubled from 1966 to 1973. All of these events contributed to a decade of uncertainty about social stability that was reflected in the prevailing mood that "something was wrong" in the society itself.

Descriptive trends and interpretations of those trends are important, but the primary concern of this study is tolerance for nonconformity. What relevance does belief in the Devil have for social and political attitudes? There are both theological and, as we shall show, empirical reasons for the linkage between belief in the Devil and intolerance of political nonconformists. Although the Devil has not been given his due by theologians, the Devil is a prominent figure in Christian belief systems, as revealed in our data. The Devil is typically viewed as a fallen angel who became the progenitor of evil. Rather than imposing evil directly on the world, he is believed to work through human agents—individuals and groups. This belief immediately raises the sociological question of who those agents are likely to be.

Historically, nonconformists have been singled out as those most vulnerable to control by evil forces and hence those most likely to become purveyors of evil (Erikson, 1966). The connection between intolerance for nonconformists and belief in the Devil that this historical fact suggests is reinforced by the data presented in Table 52.

Table 52. Tolerance Scale Score and Certainty About the Devil, 1973.

	Certain That the Devil Exists:			
Tolerance Scale Score	Percent Completely True	Percent Probably True	Percent Not True or Doubts	Number
Less tolerant	73	14	13	602
In-between	62	18	20	961
More tolerant	35	24	41	1,887

Those least tolerant of political and religious nonconformists are by far the most certain the Devil exists. Conversely, those most tolerant are least convinced of the Devil's existence.

The evidence is striking. Traditional Christians who participate actively in their churches and who find themselves with limited resources to comprehend and affect the larger world closely link God and political authority and are also highly likely to see political nonconformity as the work of the Devil. When the effects of education, gender, size of residence, participation in voluntary associations, and age are accounted for by Multiple Classification Analysis, the correlation of a combined measure of religious orthodoxy/participation and tolerance of nonconformists is .19 (without adjustments it is .35).

In a broad sense, then, religion as measured by beliefs also has a significant linkage to political attitudes. Such a syndrome, of course, does not necessarily portend a new round of witch-hunting. Attitudes and beliefs are not social actions. Social structures and changes weigh heavily on the production of behavior. What kind of political leadership emerges and what major events occur, for example, are likely to be important determinants of whether or not such beliefs would find expression and have social consequence. Demagogues have been successful in the past in activating such predisposition (Hofstadter, 1965). And even though there is impressive evidence in our study that Americans are moving toward a more tolerant, open, and finely tuned sophistication, backlashes can occur. Even if such backlashes do not occur or do not have significant social impact as a movement, the kind of religious world views we have been discussing gives rise to another concern.

In a modern world where problems are complex and solutions increasingly require careful, systematic, and reliable information and information-processing, both at the individual and at the societal levels, a world view that quickly fixates on simple and absolute certainties is not well equipped to identify collective interests or to openly gather all the relevant information—and over one-third of the populace appears to hold this kind of world view. Consequently, social problems are viewed as threats or devils to be exorcised, not as symptoms of a malfunctioning society.

The modern person is no less concerned than the anti-modernist with understanding the world and making sense of it. On

the contrary, he pursues purpose and meaning with an intensity that
Paul Pruyser (1974, p. 244) suggested is religious in its own right:

> Modern man is as interested in meaning as the people
> of old, but he has learned to run pragmatic tests of meaning.
> He makes plausible guesses and teases them out, knowing
> that these are his guesses and his tests—not the word of God.
> He raises questions, one after another. His provisional
> answers turn into new questions, in an open-ended series.
> Though he likes answers too, he is quick to discover that
> answers have limitations, for he is acutely aware of the gaps in
> knowledge. He does not mind assuming an agnostic stance,
> for he is less frightened by the hidden features of reality. He
> has tempered the animistic urge to personalize his ultimates,
> not because he has lost sensitivity to personhood and personal
> relations, but because the very idea of personhood has become
> more mysterious to him, more complex, more subtle. He can-
> not be pat about it. So he dwells on question after question,
> seeking an ever higher quality of questioning. He has new
> regard for openness—in a way, modern man is beginning to
> fear that closure may quickly deteriorate into fixity.

Chapter 9

Community Leaders
and Protection of
Democratic Principles

/\

Cumulative research findings over the past twenty years, including those obtained by Stouffer (1955), have persuaded many political observers that democracy no longer exists in American society, if in fact it ever did. Based on this evidence, a new conceptualization has arisen, called "democratic elitism." This perspective suggests that although government is not controlled by the people, it operates in their interest. Groups of political elites represent the people and preserve the fundamental principles of democracy. Although some view this optimistically, others are not so sanguine. Critics of democratic elitism fear that this system cannot succeed in the long run and that unless the people gain control over their government, democratic principles will give way to totalitarianism and individual freedoms will disappear. This chapter will examine these ideas.

Disillusionment with Democracy in American Society

Conceptions of democracy abound, and it is far beyond the scope of this book to discuss, compare, and contrast them; we are not so much concerned with a scholarly theory of democracy as we are with democratic principles that are embodied in our popular understanding of democracy in the United States.

Many of the specific principles that are currently perceived as democratic and are specified in the United States Constitution, such as freedom of speech, arise from a comparatively limited set of propositions about the proper relationship between people and their government. Paramount among these is the belief that equal weight should be given to the views of each citizen. Consequently, each person must be provided with an equal opportunity to express his or her views. Decisions must be made, of course, which leads to another fundamental principle, majority rule. But, in keeping with the principles concerning the equal importance of all citizens and their opportunity to be heard, the majority, no matter what the inclination, cannot abrogate the basic or unalienable rights of the individual. Providing an opportunity to participate in government is only a first step, however. The people must exercise this right. The government must be *by the people* to ensure that decisions will be made in their best interests, that is, decisions will be made *for the people*. Furthermore, participation *of the people* is necessary to preserve the dignity of the individual and to allow for moral and intellectual development. At the most general level, people must be willing to abide by majority decisions and to respect individual rights.

It follows from this conception of democracy that there must be widespread public support of democratic principles. Without such support either of two things could happen: the majority could suppress minority rights, or an elite could gain control of the government and subvert majority rule.

The conviction that the public did believe in and support democracy was seldom challenged before the 1950s. Perhaps the increasingly large body of evidence showing tremendous social and cultural diversity within the society caused a shift in emphasis from the idea that people shared "ideas, customs, and opinions" to the notion that they agreed on "fundamental democratic values" and the "rules of the game," but few doubted the existence of public consensus on the important matters. And there were many reasons for feeling secure in this belief. It was the people, not public officials, who took the lead in securing democratic rights for racial minorities and women, and it was the people who pushed to limit the power of economic dominants over the working class. In light of these and similar events, when isolated instances of antidemocratic sentiments or public apathy were revealed, the typical reaction was to suggest that the system was failing to provide equal opportunity to all citizens. In other words, the belief was not only that democracy could be successful, but that it was successful. The objective was simply to make it work better.

Findings from a study of voting behavior by Berelson and associates in 1954 provided one of the first important contradictions to the belief that democracy was functioning successfully in the United States. The investigators, consistent with the view prevalent at that time, did not conclude that democracy was not working. However, they were faced with the problem of reconciling this view with evidence showing that a large segment of the public was uninvolved in political affairs. They concluded that democratic theory had made the error of focusing too heavily on the individual and political consensus. A democracy needs the apathetic and marginally active as well as the politically active. To function properly, a democratic system needs sufficient heterogeneity to provide "enough consensus to hold the system together and enough cleavage to make it move" (Berelson, Lazarsfeld, and McPhee, 1954, p. 318).

Although Berelson and associates may have presented the first systematic collection of data contradicting a basic assumption of democracy, the suppression of civil liberties in the 1950s, especially that stemming from the McCarthy hearings, appears to have been responsible for the true beginning of disillusionment. Bachrach (1967, p. 29), for example, suggested that, "with the onslaught of postwar reaction and the rise of McCarthyism in America, the democratic faith in the common man, if not shattered, was subjected to serious doubt. . . . The persistent threat to freedom from these quarters was a new and frightening phenomenon. For unlike the days of the Alien and Sedition Acts and the Palmer raids, McCarthy was not vigorously opposed by any sector in the society and had the tacit approval, if not the active support, of an uncomfortably large number of people from all strata of society."

It is clear that Stouffer was among those fearful that people might be willing to sacrifice democratic rights in the name of national security. However, Stouffer clung to a belief in what he called the "sober second thought of the people"; people might act irrationally at first, but they would reaffirm their belief in democratic principles after having thought through the matter more carefully. Despite Stouffer's optimism, his research findings, like those of Berelson and associates, depicted a people with little interest in, and poorly informed about, their government. More importantly, Stouffer's study also showed that many of these individuals were unwilling to grant civil rights to persons they considered nonconformist or potentially dangerous.

During the decade following the reports by Berelson and associates and by Stouffer, a number of studies were published and provided further evidence that democracy was not functioning as well as had been believed (Mills, 1956; Kornhauser, 1959; Lipset, 1960; Campbell and others, 1960; Converse, 1964; Milbrath, 1965). To illustrate, in a 1960 study, Prothro and Grigg found considerable support for democratic principles, broadly phrased, but when these principles were reworded as specific propositions, consensus broke down. Four years later a national study by McClosky (1964) provided even more conclusive evidence of the public's lack of commitment to democratic values. Using a variety of measures, McClosky found large proportions of the population, especially those from the nation's lower socioeconomic strata, giving antidemocratic responses. His conclusion (McClosky, 1964, p. 375) is worth quoting at some length since it typifies the disillusionment of many American scholars with the feasibility of democracy:

> The findings furnish little comfort for those who wish to believe that a passion for freedom, tolerance, justice and other democratic values springs spontaneously from the lower depths of the society, and that the plain, homespun, uninitiated yeoman, worker, and farmer are the natural hosts of democratic ideology. The mystique of the simple, unworldly, "natural" democrat has been with us since at

least the rise of Christianity. . . . Usually the simpler the man, the lower his station in life, and the greater his objective need for equality, the more we have endowed him with a capacity for understanding democracy. We are thus inclined to give the nod to the farmer over the city man, the unlearned over the educated, the poor man over the man of wealth, the "people" over their leaders, the unsophisticated over the sophisticated. Yet every one of these intuitive expectations turns out, upon investigation, to be questionable or false. Democratic beliefs and habits are obviously not "natural" but must be learned; and they are learned more slowly by men and women whose lives are circumscribed by apathy, ignorance, provincialism and social or physical distance from the centers of intellectual activity. In the absence of knowledge and experience . . . the presuppositions and complex obligations of democracy, the rights it grants and the self-restraints it imposes, cannot be quickly comprehended. Even in a highly developed democratic nation like the United States, millions of people continue to possess only the most rudimentary understanding of democratic ideology.

Democratic Elitism

If research findings had simply indicated that Americans were apathetic and thus being controlled by a power elite, it could have been argued that democracy was failing by default. However, the findings from studies, such as those by Stouffer, Prothro and Grigg, and McClosky cited earlier, suggested that *greater political activity by the people could very well undermine democracy rather than strengthen it.* An attempt to resolve this apparent dilemma produced the theory of "democratic elitism." Given that the public contains a high proportion of apathetic and antidemocratic people, then the first question to be resolved was whether democratic principles continue to be operative in American society.

In addition to his study of the rank and file, Stouffer sampled the opinions of civic leaders in cities throughout the United States. His findings showed that leaders tended to be more tolerant than the rest of the population. Although disappointed with the generally low levels of political tolerance, he felt this finding offered hope for the preservation of democratic principles. Stouffer (1955, p. 57) put it this way: "From various points of view, the detailed attitudes reported in this chapter—even the attitudes of civic leaders—may not be a pleasant picture. But the fact that responsible community leaders are more likely than the rank and file to give the sober second thought to the civil rights of the nonconformists or suspected nonconformists here studied can be of much significance to America's future. If the reverse had been found, the future might look dark indeed to those who view with anxiety current threats to historic liberties." McClosky (1964, p. 374) reached a conclusion similar to Stouffer's on the basis of his findings from a sample of delegates and alternates who attended the 1956 Democratic and Republican conventions: "The evidence suggests that it is the articulate classes rather than the public who serve as the major repositories of the public conscience and as carriers of the Creed. Responsibility for keeping the system going, hence, falls most heavily upon them." This view was widely accepted among political theorists and became one of the basic propositions of democratic elitism. Put another way, democratic elitism holds that political decisions generally adhere to fundamental democratic values and are made according to democratic rules of procedure because political leaders continue to support democratic principles.

Once political theorists determined that democratic principles continue to operate through political leaders, another question became immediately apparent. Since the public contains many people with antidemocratic sentiments, and since many leaders are publicly elected, what prevents the election of leaders who do not support democratic values? From the perspective of democratic elitism, the answer is twofold. First, members of the middle and upper classes tend to be more involved and active in public affairs than are members of the lower and working classes, and they command far more resources advantageous to attaining positions of political power. Consequently, they are much more likely to be elected to office. Thus, leadership positions are generally filled by persons supporting democratic values. Second, even when antidemocratic people become leaders, which obviously happens on occasion, their attitudes tend to change. According to the theory, the society has a distinctive political stratum, which resocializes new members into its own cultural orientation. Key (1961), for example, suggested that political newcomers are indoctrinated into the norms of a politically active subculture, and Dahl (1961), although recognizing that middle- and upper-class persons are more likely to support democratic rules of the game, suggested that the greater support from political leaders comes from being socialized into politics as well. This distinctive political stratum is said to arise from and to be perpetuated by the unavoidable exposure of leaders to the nation's democratic heritage and by the necessity of applying those principles in a reasonably coherent and consistent manner. Members of the public, who are less aware of the diverse needs and conflicting interests of the society's heterogeneous population, imagine that they can live their lives without having to concern themselves with decisions which greatly affect the welfare of others. Leaders, whether in public office or in voluntary associations, must make decisions, and they need a set of principles to aid them in the process. Democratic principles, including the rule of democratic restraint, are readily available within America's cultural tradition.

According to democratic elitism, the threat of exploitation of the public by the elite may be blunted, perhaps prevented altogether, by their commitment to democratic values. However, the theory typically has been merged with another perspective, often referred to as "political pluralism" (see Riesman, 1950; Dahl, 1954; Jackman, 1972). This view proposes that even though leaders may share a belief in the democratic rules of the game, they differ considerably on other issues. In this sense, there is not one elite, but many. These elite groups are said to represent the diverse interests of the people and to depend on the people for political support. Thus, each segment of the society, such as farmers, labor, minorities, women, business, and consumers, is represented by an elite. According to this view, the diverse interests and overlapping constituencies of the elite tend to prevent any one group of elites from gaining an excess of power.

Examining the Propositions of Democratic Elitism

Does American society have a democratic system of government, as that term is popularly conceived, or does it have something else? Are the proponents of democratic elitism correct; that is, do we have a government for the people, but not of and by them? Perhaps both views are inaccurate; perhaps American government comes closer to elite rule governed by principles contrary to democratic principles and inconsistent with the interests of the people, as writers such as Mills (1956) and events like the Watergate affair have suggested. With these questions in mind, let us examine the propositions of democratic elitism* using our data collected from American civic leaders living in cities with populations of 10,000 to 150,000.

The first proposition discussed above was that, despite a considerable amount of antidemocratic sentiment in the national population, leaders tend to share a common commitment to democratic principles. This idea can be examined by using Stouffer's Tolerance Scale. The scale does not measure attitudes toward all democratic principles, of course, but support of civil liberties is most certainly at the core of democratic values. Table 53 shows the distribution of

Table 53. Tolerance Scale Scores by Community Leaders and National Cross Section in Cities and in Rural and Urban Areas.

Tolerance Scale Score	Community Leaders:		Cross Section in Cities, 10,000–150,000:		Cross Section, Rural and Urban:	
	Percent	Number	Percent	Number	Percent	Number
Less tolerant						
0	1	6	5	56	5	196
1	3	18	9	103	10	357
In-between						
2	6	37	13	151	15	529
3	8	50	12	135	14	503
More tolerant						
4	16	101	15	170	15	520
5	67	437	45	514	41	1,441
Total	100	649	100	1,129	100	3,546

*It must be pointed out that neither democratic elitism nor earlier theories of democracy have been articulated in quantitatively specific terms. Thus, for example, it has been suggested that democracy is dependent on widespread public consensus on democratic values, but it is not clear exactly how much consensus is required. Presumably, both democratic theory and democratic elitism conceive of governmental types as arrayed along a continuum, such that any concrete or real system more or less approximates a particular form of government. This type of theory construction is preferable to less realistic "all or none" propositions, but it nevertheless forces problems in data interpretation. Therefore, determination of the validity of the propositions examined here rests partly on each individual's intuitive conception of the relationship between quantitative findings and a particular kind of political system.

leader scores compared with those in the national population and with persons living in cities of the same size as those from which the sample of leaders was drawn. As can be seen, although all three groups contain people with scores from the least tolerant to the most tolerant on the scale, leaders are much more likely than the rank and file to have scores indicating support for democratic values. With 83 percent of the leaders classified as more tolerant, it seems reasonable to conclude that community leaders, at least of the "grass roots" type sampled in this study, do in fact tend to share a common commitment to democratic values.

One might ask whether this endorsement of democratic principles applies to all types of civic leaders or just to some of them. Of course we cannot answer this question for types of leaders not included in the survey, but among the fourteen different categories of leaders we studied, only one, commanders of the American Legion, equalled the national population in the proportion more tolerant. All the other types exceeded this average, some by more than 40 percentage points.

Recall that a partial explanation given by the proponents of democratic elitism for the commitment of leaders to democratic values is that they tend to come from the ranks of the middle and upper classes—strata which are more likely to support these principles. Data from the present study are consistent with this proposition. Seventy-five percent of the leaders are either in business (managers, proprietors, or officials) or in professional occupations. Only 22 percent of the national cross section fall into these categories. Of the national cross section, 31 percent are blue-collar workers compared to 8 percent of the leaders. Over half, 54 percent, of the leaders completed college and another 22 percent received some college training. Of the rank and file, only 16 percent are college graduates, and 18 percent have some college education. Only 5 percent of the community leaders did not graduate from high school, compared to 35 percent of the rank and file.

Although the findings show that community leaders tend to come from the ranks of the middle and upper classes, some clearly have their origins in America's lower strata. According to democratic elitism, if these persons bring antidemocratic sentiments with them, and are not resocialized into supporting democratic principles, then their presence in the elite might disrupt the functioning of a democratic system. Furthermore, since not all members of the upper strata are sympathetic to democratic values, resocialization of these individuals might be necessary as well.

Ideally, the idea of resocialization should be examined through a longitudinal study, measuring first the attitudes of persons when they first become members of the political elite and then monitoring any changes in these attitudes. This procedure cannot be used with the data from the present study, but we can use another method to validate or invalidate the existence of a distinctive political stratum. If persons are resocialized into accepting democratic principles through their experiences in a unique political stratum, then leaders should be more supportive of democratic values than their social-status counterparts who are not leaders.

At least three studies have used this general approach. Using data from four Wisconsin cities, Alford and Scoble (1968) attempted to measure the relative effect of leadership and social status on political attitudes and behavior. Both variables were found to be independently associated with tolerance, but social status, as indexed by education, had the larger effect. The second study, by Jackman (1972), used Stouffer's data. Jackman's procedure was more rigorous than the approach used by Alford and Scoble in that he attempted to compare the tolerance of leaders and of the public within categories of education after controlling for the effects of gender, region, and city size. The findings led him to conclude that there is no distinctive political stratum. It appears, however, that an error in analysis may have led Jackman to this conclusion. St. Peter, Williams, and Johnson (1977) reanalyzed the data and found that leadership continued to have a significant effect on tolerance after holding the other variables constant. The third study was conducted by Comer and Welch (1975) in a midwestern city. Elite status was found to have an effect on ideology and tolerance after removing the effects of education and party identification.

Examination of the data from the present study began with a variable-by-variable approach comparing leaders with other persons living in cities of the same size as those lived in by the leaders. Singly, gender, region, exposure to the mass media, city size, occupation, and education failed to eliminate the tolerance difference between leaders and the public. In combination, however, these variables accounted for the difference. That is, on Stouffer's Tolerance Scale, which has a range of 0 (lowest tolerance) to 5 (highest tolerance), people living in cities with 10,000 to 150,000 population have an average score of 3.63, and the leaders have a score of 4.36. After controlling for the effects of the aforementioned variables, the difference was reduced to nonsignificance. (See Andrews and others, 1973, for a discussion of the method.) A comparison of each type of leader with the public produced the same finding. Thus, at least at the community level, a unique political stratum no longer exists in American society.

The proposition that leaders represent diverse societal interests is one of the propositions of democratic elitism that most importantly distinguishes it from a purely elitist theory. The people may be apathetic and uninvolved in the political process, but their interests are protected and supported by groups of elites. In addition to their acceptance of democratic principles, representation of these divergent public interests prevents leaders from possibly recognizing their common interests as elites and thus reduces the likelihood of their uniting to exploit the public. Support for this pluralist position would be obtained if types of leaders were found to differ in their concern about a particular issue. Even greater support would be evident if differential concern among leader types was found for different issues. To this end, four distinct topics—crime, high prices, pollution, and poverty—were chosen for analysis. For each topic, leaders were asked whether it was a serious threat, moderate threat, or not a threat to the United States. Table 54 shows the extent to which different kinds of leaders view these issues as serious threats to the nation. There is not a great deal of difference among most of the leader types in regard to crime. However, as might be expected from the perspective of political pluralism, police chiefs are much more likely than any other kind of leader to view crime as a serious threat. It will be recalled that the Republican party identified itself as representing the interests of "law and order" in the 1972 presidential election. Thus, further support is given to the pluralist position when we find Republican county central committee chairpeople as more likely to see crime as a threat than their Democratic counterparts. Public officials do not differ greatly among themselves on the issue of high prices, but some marked differences in perception do occur among some of the other types of lead-

Table 54. Perception of Crime, High Prices, Pollution, and Poverty as Serious Threats to the United States, by Type of Leader.

Type of Leader	Percent Answering Serious Threat:				
	Crime	High Prices	Pollution	Poverty	Number[a]
Public officials					
Mayors	77	63	43	32	48
Police chiefs	91	61	41	29	44
Presidents, school board	62	64	45	31	50
Presidents, library board	69	60	69	38	45
Political party chairpeople					
Republican county central committee	79	59	39	19	39
Democratic county central committee	64	71	55	39	43
Industrial leaders					
Presidents, chamber of commerce	77	75	35	32	50
Presidents, labor union	76	82	70	58	45
Voluntary groups					
Presidents, League of Women Voters	63	46	75	54	48
Presidents, PTA	68	80	77	36	51
Presidents, bar association	64	60	35	15	49
Chairpeople, United Fund	73	58	48	17	49
Commanders, American Legion	64	67	46	18	40
Other					
Newspaper publishers	67	76	38	20	47

[a]Numbers vary slightly from issue to issue because of an occasional nonresponse.

ers. Presidents of labor unions, presumably representing the interests of the working class, top the list of concerned leaders, with 82 percent saying that high prices represent a serious threat. Traditionally, the

Democratic party has been billed as supporting the interests of America's working class and poor, whereas the Republican party has been associated with the society's upper class and "big business." The findings are consistent with this view. Seventy-one percent of the Democratic party leaders perceive high prices as a serious threat, compared to 59 percent of the Republican officials. It is difficult to interpret the high percentage among PTA presidents saying that high prices are a threat. A possible explanation is that many of them are women, who, in this case, are not responding to the question as PTA representatives but as consumers directly facing the impact of inflation in 1973 through, for example, the soaring prices of groceries. However, it is difficult to reconcile this interpretation with the relatively small percentage found among presidents of the League of Women Voters. The distribution of attitudes toward pollution and poverty shows even more pronounced differences among leaders than the issues of crime and high prices. In regard to pollution, the two largest percentages, those from presidents of the PTA and League of Women Voters, are more than double those of presidents of bar associations and the Chamber of Commerce. The overall pattern of responses to the seriousness of pollution is supportive of the suggestion that leaders associated with business or industrial interests, or dependent on these interests, such as the Chamber of Commerce, corporate lawyers, newspaper publishers, and representatives of the Republican party, are less likely than many others to see pollution as a serious threat to the nation. Business and industry, of course, are among the major sources of pollution problems. Groups more oriented toward the interests of the public at large, such as presidents of library boards, Democratic party officials, labor union presidents, presidents of the League of Women Voters and of the PTA, on the other hand, are more likely to define pollution as a serious threat. Consistent with the proposition that certain types of leaders represent the interests of the working and lower classes, presidents of labor unions, Democratic officials, and presidents of the League of Women Voters are the most likely to view poverty as a serious threat. The percentages obtained from these leaders are about three times larger than those of leaders less directly linked to these interests, such as presidents of bar associations, commanders of the American Legion, and Republican officials.

For present purposes, the accuracy of the interpretations of leader differences is less important than the simple fact that different types of leaders differ in their attitudes toward various social issues. The marked differences among leader types found here would seem to provide support for the pluralist conception of democratic elitism.

The Future of American Democracy

Although far from being definitive, the data in this and other studies suggest that the concept of democratic elitism describes the operation of government in the United States. Such a finding does not mean that it is the only system possible or necessarily the most preferable. Of course, defining the most desirable system of government, even within scientifically determined limits of the possible, cannot be accomplished through empirical procedures. However, democratic elitism can be evaluated within the framework of America's long-standing expression of democratic objectives.

Both previous research and the present study suggest that a large segment of America's public is uninvolved and uninterested in the political process and that a sizable proportion hold antidemocratic values. Nevertheless, despite this lack of involvement and lack of commitment to democratic principles, the diverse interests of the people appear to be represented by political elites. And, even though these leaders support different and sometimes conflicting interests, they tend to share a common, supportive attitude toward democratic values. Their consensus apparently is maintained through recruitment of leaders from the nation's middle and upper classes (but no longer through resocialization). In short, exploitation of the masses is believed to be prevented by the presence of multiple elites with different interests and a common commitment to democratic principles. The subversion of democratic values by an antidemocratic public is prevented by elite control of the government and by the apathy of the people. On the basis of these considerations, some political theorists have argued that democratic elitism is the most desirable system of government possible in modern society. Milbrath (1965, p. 154), for example, stated that "present levels and patterns of participation in politics do not constitute a threat to democracy; they seem, in fact, to be a realistic adjustment to the nature of modern society. The political processes of that democracy may not be close to the ideal of the classical theorists, but they may well be the best possible approximation to popular control of government that can be achieved in modern, industrialized, mobile, mass society."

On the other hand, other theorists, a minority, have suggested that the present system falls short of meeting vital democratic objectives. Whereas Milbrath vigorously defended the importance of "moderate" public participation in government, Bachrach (1967, p. 106) just as vigorously took the opposite view: "If it is time to abandon the myth of the common man's allegiance to democracy, it is also time that elites in general and political scientists in particular recognize that without the common man's active support, liberty cannot be preserved over the long run. The battle for freedom will be lost by default if elites insulate themselves from the people and rely on countervailing forces, institutional and social barriers, and their own colleagues to defend the system from the demagogic leaders of the mob. Democracy can best be assured of survival by enlisting the people's support in a continual effort to make democracy meaningful in the lives of all men."

Criticisms of democratic elitism appear to be based largely, although not exclusively, on three points. First, it is argued that the dependency of the people on elites to protect their interests creates a serious risk of elitist exploitation. The political structure may be pluralistic, but some elites are far more powerful than others. Thus, political pluralism is no guarantee that all interests will be equally represented or even that all interests will be represented (see Kornhauser, 1966). That public interests and the rights of the individual can be disregarded and abused by public officials became vividly clear with the discoveries leading to the Watergate affair. Subsequent evidence concerning illegal activities by the FBI and CIA did nothing to restore public confidence in the integrity of the nation's leaders. Second, by having greater access to agents of persuasion, such as the mass media and the flow of information, elites can manipulate the perceived interests of the people. Consequently, people can be fooled into believing they want something that is in reality against their own interests. Finally, without full and active participation, that is, without government of and by the people, the dignity of the individual is disregarded and the opportunity for moral and intellectual development is preempted by the elite (see Erbe, 1964; Aberback, 1969; Zurcher, 1970; Pateman, 1970).

If the opposing views of democratic elitists and their critics rested solely on differences in values, then an empirical reconciliation would be impossible. But the advocates of democratic elitism do not claim that this system of government is ideal, but rather that it is the most desirable system *under present societal conditions*. Thus, although the advocates tend to be considerably more confident about the built-in protections of the system, its checks and balances, than their opponents, both sides appear to agree that democratic elitism does provide a reasonably accurate picture of the way government currently operates in American society. The contention revolves around the feasibility of alternatives. Let us examine the ideas relating to this contention.

It has been argued that full public participation in the political decision-making process is impossible in a nation with a highly diversified and complex division of labor and a population of more than 214,000,000 people. On the face of it, this seems to be an indisputable fact, if by "full participation" one uses a small New England town in the eighteenth century as a model. It is quite clear, however, that many more people could be active in public affairs than are. Size and complexity may discourage some people from public participation, but they do not structurally preclude a great number of politically oriented activities, such as voting, membership in voluntary associations, keeping informed about current events, contributing to campaigns with time or money, writing letters to newspapers and public officials, attending public hearings, signing petitions, running for office, and engaging in peaceful demonstrations. In fact, there are probably many areas in which citizens could be more fully involved than they are now in actual planning processes leading to political decisions, such as devising plans for urban development and redevelopment, developing objectives for public education, and devising programs to assist the physically handicapped. (See Pateman, 1970, for example, for some interesting ideas regarding participatory democracy in industry.) Participation in these activities would not guarantee that each individual will have an equal voice in the political process, but it would provide persons with more opportunity to express their views and to have a larger impact on governmental decisions.

A second idea is that a high level of citizen participation, with a high degree of interest, could produce deep cleavages within the population, making resolution of issues extremely difficult, if not impossible (Berelson, Lazarsfeld, and McPhee, 1954; Almond and Verba, 1963). This position, however, appears to be predicated on another concern, the possibility that people will be unwilling to abide by democratic principles or that they will constitute a tyranny of the majority. Given the combination of active citizen participation and widespread antidemocratic sentiments, people might attempt to deny civil liberties, especially to persons who thought or behaved in a disapproved manner. It is this issue that seems to pose the most serious dilemma for the future of democracy in American society. What would happen to democratic institutions and values if people were more involved? What would prevent them from destroying the principles on which American democracy is based?

If an atheist had been invited to make a speech in the spring of 1954 and the matter had been put to a vote, it is likely that the speech would have been forbidden. Based on Stouffer's data, 63 percent of the adult population would have voted not to allow it. If the same situation had arisen in the spring of 1973, the vote would have gone the other way; only 36 percent would have voted not to allow it. This illustrates a finding that has been thoroughly documented in preceding chapters: the dramatic increase in public support for democratic principles. Stouffer (1955, p. 236) suggested that "great social, economic, and technological forces are operating slowly and imperceptibly on the side of spreading tolerance." We have seen many of these forces at work. The population has become far more educated, moving from a majority in 1954 who never graduated from high school to a nation in 1973 where the high school graduate was commonplace and more than one of every three adults had attended college. Rural to urban migration occurred throughout this period, with a significant buildup in metropolitan areas. The proportion of men and women employed in white collar occupations increased, while the proportions in unskilled and semiskilled jobs declined. These and other changes in the social and demographic composition of the American public have produced the response Stouffer anticipated.

Given the substantial increase in public support for democratic principles, the risk of demagogic takeover or the undermining of civil liberties is less now than it once was. Antidemocratic attitudes are still widespread among people, and the nation's leaders continue to play an important role in protecting individual rights and other democratic values. But the difference between the values of civic leaders and the public is not as great as it was in 1954, and the current difference is primarily caused by the increased tolerance of leaders. The increase in the proportion more tolerant among comparable leaders from 1954 to 1973 was 66 to 82 percent. It would be foolish, projecting from the change that occurred between 1954 and 1973, to suggest that the general public will equal the leaders in tolerance by the year 2009, at which time everyone will be among the more tolerant. There are simply too many unknown variables to allow for a projection with this sort of precision. However, a continuation of present trends promises greater public support for democratic principles in the years ahead. As a consequence, attempting to approximate democracy may become increasingly feasible.

If the factors contributing to support for democratic values were independent of political participation, then it might follow from the considerations discussed above that democratic elitism should be maintained at the present, even if government of and by the people is considered a desirable objective. However, the entire theoretical and empirical thrust of the material presented here and in other chapters indicates that this would be an inaccurate conclusion. In their struggle for civil rights, members of minorities have often been told to be patient, that they are not yet ready to assume the full rights and responsibilities of first-class citizenship. Social scientists have generally recognized this caution for what it is, a rationalization designed by members of the majority to protect their advantaged position. But from the perspective of many investigators working in the area of race and ethnic relations, such a rationalization provides only part of the explanation. Majority persons do not realize that certain of the minority characteristics which they define as undesirable *stem from* the disadvantages of minority status. Advocates of democratic elitism, albeit unintentionally, may be perpetuating the same fallacy. McClosky (1964, p. 374), for example, suggested that "political apathy seems for most men the more 'natural state.'" When explaining why leaders tend to be more supportive of democratic principles than the public, he (p. 372) states that "political involvement heightens one's sense of intellectual order and commitment." McClosky (p. 374) then attempts to reconcile these views by proposing that "inarticulates . . . are inclined to avoid the very activities by which they might overcome their indifference and develop a more coherent point of view." Of course, if apathy is indeed a "natural state," then democracy is impossible. We suggest, however, that apathy, ignorance, antidemocratic attitudes, and the other characteristics of the public that have been used to justify democratic elitism are no more "natural" for most people than they are for black people, women, the poor, or any other population. Instead, we submit that these characteristics are the result of structural and organizational components of society. A dramatic increase in political tolerance among Americans from 1954 to 1973 has been shown in the present study. A variable (in this case tolerance) cannot be explained by a constant, and a "natural state" is a constant.

Given that participatory democracy is a desirable goal, increasing the opportunities for public involvement and encouraging people to participate in their government need not result in the downfall of democracy. The act of participation will itself contribute to promoting understanding, appreciation, and support of democratic values. Articulate, knowledgeable people may realistically fear temporary setbacks on particular issues with increased public participation in governmental processes, just as some men have had to suffer "reverse discrimination" in certain instances while sexual equality is being established. But such temporary setbacks would appear to be the short-term costs in a long-term struggle for liberty.

Chapter 10

Tolerance and Sociopolitical Activity

/\\.\\/\\.\\/\\.\\/\\.\\/\\.\\/\\.\\/\\.\\/\\.\\/\\.\\/\\.\\/\\.\\/\\.\\/\\.\\/\\.\\/\\.\\/\\.\\/\\.\\/\\

Stouffer's (1955) Tolerance Scale was composed of questions asking people how they would feel if certain situations arose, such as: *"Now I should like to ask you some questions about a man who admits he is a Communist. Suppose this admitted Communist wants to make a speech in your community. Should he be allowed to speak or not?"* These scale questions, and the related questions we have used to measure tolerance, do not measure behavior. They do not even ask the respondent what he or she might do under the circumstances. Yet we know that some people are much more likely than others to become actively involved in community and national affairs. For example, two people, both against allowing an admitted Communist to speak in their community, might act quite differently: One might attempt to prevent the speech from taking place, and the other might do nothing.

Stouffer sought to rectify this problem in two ways. First, he drew a sample of community leaders and asked them the same questions that he put to the national cross section. It was assumed that the leaders were active people; otherwise they would not have been in positions of leadership. Second, he divided his sample of the national population into two groups, the "more interested" and the "less interested." People were asked: *"Frequently there is something in the news about Communists in the United States and what is being done about them. On the whole, would you say you follow this news very closely, fairly closely, or hardly at all?"* Those answering "very closely" or "fairly closely" were called the "more interested." These persons were shown to be more likely to read a daily newspaper, to listen to news programs on radio and television, to be informed about current events, and to have voted in the 1952 presidential election. Stouffer (1955, pp. 85–86) concluded: "It is upon the attitudes of the 'more interested' group that we shall focus our main attention. Such people are more likely than others to include among them those who are influential, or outspoken, or reflective, or active, and who are more likely to translate an opinion into action, whatever their station in life."

The influence of public opinion polling has increased tremendously in the past twenty years. Through national surveys, political officials and other leaders are made aware of public attitudes on nearly every important issue. Consequently, in the 1970s people can and do have an impact on policy without having to stir from their living rooms. Nevertheless, the increased importance of opinion polling does not mean that the importance of action has diminished. We are all familiar with the potential power of such activities as voting, strikes, boycotts, marches, and petitions. Thus, it is still useful to consider the attitudes of the more active people in the society, even if separating them from less active citizens is not as crucial as it once was.

In preceding chapters, we presented evidence showing that civic leaders tend to be more tolerant than the national cross section. Leaders appear to be the primary guardians of civil liberties and other democratic values. In Chapter Nine it also was proposed that in the long run, democracy cannot stand without an interested, informed, and active populace. Many political observers have expressed a concern that antidemocratic sentiments in the public could undermine democratic institutions if the public were to become more active. Chapter Nine concluded with the suggestion that this fear may be unfounded, that it is the exposure to social and cultural diversity brought about through participation in the society which promotes understanding and appreciation of democratic principles. Thus, we should find that the more interested, that is, the more active, are also the more tolerant. This is the proposition examined in the present chapter.

Interest in Current Events

As we mentioned, Stouffer measured interest in current events by asking people how closely they followed news about Communists. When his study was conducted, it would have been difficult to be exposed to mass media news without being exposed to news about Communists, a fact that was not true in 1973. Hence, in our survey we asked a different question, designed to measure the same underlying dimension of interest in current affairs: *"Frequently there is something in the news on such topics as war protestors, campus unrest, women's liberation movement, and black militants. On the whole, would you say you follow this news very closely, fairly closely, or hardly at all?"* The percentage distribution of responses to this question is almost identical to the one obtained by Stouffer. Following his procedure, we combined the percentages answering "very closely" and "fairly closely," which yielded a total of 58 percent characterized as more interested. Stouffer's total was 56 percent. Specific responses to our question were as follows: 11 percent, "very closely"; 47 percent, "fairly closely"; and 40 percent, "hardly at all." Two percent said they did not know. Table 55 shows that the more interested, both in 1954 and in 1973, also tend to be the more tolerant using Stouffer's Tolerance Scale.*

The 1973 survey also included several questions dealing with interest in current events apart from those pertaining to mass media exposure. First, respondents were asked about their interest in local

---

*It seemed possible that our question about following the news closely measured interest only in the topics used as illustrations. To check for this possibility, we performed additional analysis, which showed that the frequency of listening to news programs on television and reading newspapers, magazines, and books was positively associated with tolerance.

Table 55. Tolerance Scale Score and Interest in Current Events,
National Cross Section, 1954 and 1973.

| | Tolerance Scale Scores: | | | |
Interest in Current Events	Percent Less Tolerant	Percent In- Between	Percent More Tolerant	Number
1954				
More interested	16	48	36	2,778
Less interested	23	52	25	2,076
1973				
More interested	12	26	62	2,074
Less interested	19	34	47	1,399

and national politics. As expected, the greater the interest, the larger
the percentage scoring high on the Tolerance Scale. In reference to
local politics, 57 percent of the more interested scored as more tolerant, compared to 47 percent of the less interested. The relationship is
stronger for interest in national politics: 66 percent of the more interested scored as more tolerant, while only 33 percent of the less interested fell into this category.

Second, people were asked: *"Has a friend or acquaintance
recently asked your opinion about social or political issues?"* and
*"Compared to others belonging to your circle of friends, are you more
or less likely to be asked for your opinions on social and political
issues?"* Although we believe most respondents gave truthful answers
to these questions, it does not matter here whether those answering
"yes" to the first question and "more" to the second are providing
accurate information. What is relevant is that these responses indicate
having a strong enough interest in social and political issues to want
others to value their opinions. Seventy-three percent of those indicating that they were recently asked their opinion were characterized as
more tolerant, compared to 45 percent who answered "no." Among
those who said that they were more likely than their friends to be
asked for their opinion about social and political issues, 69 percent
were among the more tolerant, compared to 47 percent who answered
that they were less likely to be asked. Those who answered "same" (no
more and no less likely than others to be asked) to this question fall in
between, with 57 percent scoring as more tolerant on the scale.

Social and Political Participation

In addition to measuring interest in current events, the 1973 survey asked people about their participation in social and political organizations. Belonging to a voluntary association is itself a measure of activity, but research also shows that participation in such groups enhances the likelihood of other forms of action, such as voting, involvement in political campaigns, and trying to bring about social reform (see Lipset, Trow, and Coleman, 1956; Almond and Verba, 1963; Rose, 1967; and Sallach, Babchuk, and Booth, 1972). Association with others is a catalyst for further involvement. Thus, membership in voluntary associations is an excellent measure of active participation in the society in general.

Membership was measured through a technique known as aided recall. Rather than relying on the memories of respondents, each was provided with a list of examples of organizations appropriate to a specific category. To illustrate, group names such as Masons, Eastern Star, Lions, and Rotary were mentioned in relation to fraternal/service organizations, and suggestions such as bowling league and card club were cited in relation to recreational associations.

Table 56 shows that belonging to an organization is positively associated with tolerance for all types of groups, with the exception of church-related organizations. The category "other" includes such organizations as adult leaders of youth programs, veterans organizations, and board members of community agencies.

The data on participation in voluntary associations also can be analyzed by classifying respondents by the number of memberships they hold in different kinds of organizations. Since membership in different sorts of organizations will tend to increase a person's exposure to, and experience in, dealing with social and cultural diversity, we would expect multiple memberships to be associated with greater tolerance. As can be seen from Table 57, this expectation is strongly supported.

Summary of Findings

The findings presented in this chapter appear to offer additional encouragement to those concerned about the protection of civil liberties in the United States. Previous chapters showed a marked

Table 56. Tolerance Scale Score and Membership in
Voluntary Associations, National Cross Section, 1973.

| | *Tolerance Scale Scores:* | | | |
Membership by Type of Association	*Percent Less Tolerant*	*Percent In-Between*	*Percent More Tolerant*	*Number*
Job-related				
Belong	7	20	73	751
Not belong	18	32	50	2,792
Recreational				
Belong	9	23	68	653
Not belong	17	31	52	2,890
Fraternal/service				
Belong	10	23	67	511
Not belong	17	30	53	3,032
Civic/political				
Belong	11	22	67	477
Not belong	16	30	53	3,066
Church-related				
Belong	17	35	48	995
Not belong	15	27	58	2,546
Other				
Belong	9	20	70	358
Not belong	16	30	54	3,183

Table 57. Tolerance Scale Score and Multiple-Group Membership,
National Cross Section, 1973.

| | *Tolerance Scale Scores:* | | | |
Number of Memberships in Different Types of Organizations	*Percent Less Tolerant*	*Percent In-Between*	*Percent More Tolerant*	*Number*
0	20	33	47	1,373
1	15	30	55	1,195
2	11	25	64	573
3	12	21	68	257
4 or more	5	21	74	148

increase over the past two decades in the percentage of Americans
willing to tolerate legal nonconformity. The findings presented here
show not only that Americans have become more tolerant but also
that the most active segment of the public is the most tolerant.

Chapter 11

Political Tolerance
and American Society

/\\

We have taken a look into the "window of the American mind," as Paul Sheatsley once described Stouffer's 1954 McCarthy-era study of the American commitment to civil liberties. Taking advantage of Stouffer's earlier study, we were able to look at political tolerance in contemporary America and to compare these results with those of Stouffer almost two decades ago. Comparable methodologies of the 1954 and 1973 studies allowed us to look at nationwide samples of the general public and community leaders to see how they were changing in their willingness to extend civil liberties to nonconformists. We then probed for some of the reasons why attitudes might be changing.

What we found was not always surprising, but the results of the studies serve as bench marks for important social and psychological changes in American society. Briefly, let us review the major findings of the study. The 1954 and 1973 studies were spawned from a concern with what appeared to be a climate of fear in the society. In 1954, the Communists and the anti-Communist activities of Senator Joseph McCarthy were the focal concern. In 1973, reactions to major events of the 1960s, protest movements and the Vietnam War, suggested that Americans might be willing to trade their civil liberties

167

for law and order. We found, however, as did Stouffer, that there was
no national anxiety neurosis. Americans in 1954 and 1973 were for
the most part optimistic and did not worry a lot more than they did in
the past. By 1973, Communists and World War II had subsided as salient topics of conversation. When respondents were asked to specify
what they worried about, personal and family matters headed the
list. On the other hand, civil liberties in general or in regard to themselves were not burning concerns. If one probed a little more, however, drugs, crime, high prices, taxes, and environmental pollution
were definitely seen as serious threats to society. Could we then expect
that this lack of concern would lead citizens to be less willing to tolerate nonconformists? At best, could we expect that respondents' apathy about civil liberties would show up in our study as little or no
change in tolerance and support of civil liberties?

The answer to these questions, according to the 1954, 1973, and
more recent surveys, is that Americans' commitments to civil liberties' principles are changing, generally in a more libertarian direction. According to the fifteen-item Tolerance Scale used by Stouffer in
1954 and by us in the 1973 study, there has been a substantial shift
toward more tolerance of ideological nonconformists. In 1954, 31 percent of the general public and 66 percent of the community leaders
were classified as more tolerant. By 1973, 54 percent of the general
public and 83 percent of the leaders were classified as more tolerant.
Other indicators of support for civil liberties tell a similar story. Surveys in 1972 through 1976 generally showed a gradual increase in tolerance of Communists, Socialists, atheists, and homosexuals. These
findings are especially important because they indicate that tolerance
extends beyond the more traditional nonconformists, such as Communists, to a type of nonconformist that has only recently been in the
public spotlight. Disapproval of government wiretapping has also
shown dramatic shifts, most likely due to Watergate effects. In 1973,
44 percent disapproved of government wiretaps; by 1974, and again in
1975, 80 percent of adult Americans said that they disapproved of
wiretapping.

While most indicators showed great continuity, one area
showed results inconsistent with overall patterns: commitments to
academic freedom lagged behind other areas of individual freedom.
Americans were less willing to tolerate ideological nonconformists in

their colleges. In 1973, according to the Tolerance Scale, strong support of academic freedom was characteristic of less than a majority. Furthermore, comparisons of nationwide surveys from 1972 to 1977 showed that tolerance of homosexual professors declined during that time. And, although a majority in 1976 (49 percent in 1977) would be willing to allow a homosexual to teach in a college, less than a majority would tolerate Communist or atheist professors. This indication, plus the fact that the Tolerance Scale questions—items about Communists, Socialists, and atheists—are highly correlated with tolerance questions regarding homosexuals, suggest that the Tolerance Scale has greater generality than Stouffer himself assumed when he first used it in 1954.

After taking a look into the "window of the American mind" and seeing that, for the most part, Americans are increasingly respecting the civil liberties of their fellow citizens, we considered the more difficult question of why attitudes are changing (or not changing, as was the case for a small but not insignificant number of American people). The evidence of increasing tolerance drawn from nationwide surveys made at two points in time suggested that changes have been gradual (about 1 percent more tolerant each year) and unidirectional, but without repeated surveys between 1954 and 1973 we cannot be sure. However, National Opinion Research Center surveys that included tolerance questions identical to some of those used in the 1954 and 1973 surveys generally showed small, gradual shifts toward greater tolerance. The trend data suggest that there are some strong and persistent forces in American society that have a net effect of encouraging tolerance. In his 1954 study, Stouffer interpreted his data as indications of just such powerful forces. Foremost among these forces was education.

In the 1973 replication of the Stouffer study, we too found education to be the single most powerful predictor of tolerance. In a step-like pattern, the more education respondents had, the greater their willingness to extend civil liberties to nonconformists and the greater their support for civil liberties. On the downscale side of the education ladder were those with grade school education, of whom only 19 percent were classified as more tolerant. At the other extreme, 84 percent of the college graduates scored as more tolerant.

The education and tolerance association was strong in 1954

and in 1973, but by 1973 education had become even more closely associated with political tolerance, primarily because greater shifts took place among the more educated. While the college educated showed an increase in the proportion more tolerant of nearly 20 percent, the increase for those with grade school education in 1954 and 1973 was only 5 percent. Paradoxically, the lowest educational attainment group also increased in the proportion less tolerant by 7 percent.

Although education's impact on tolerance is straightforward and strong, education does not necessarily neutralize other forces at work on tolerance levels. Greater formal training appears to go a long way toward increasing ability to cope with a complex world, including a mixture of different kinds of people, but such considerations as political climate can complicate and, in some instances, reduce the effect of education on political attitudes such as tolerance. Yet even in a period when the political climate was fraught with concern about Communists, Stouffer found education to be highly associated with the Tolerance Scale.

What is it about education that gives it such potency to affect tolerance levels? We found that it was not the status-conferring qualities of greater education that accounted for education's impact, but those qualities that promote knowledge, a flexible cognitive style, and a broadened cultural sophistication.

As we continued our search for the sources of tolerance, we turned to age as a likely candidate. The pattern was much like that of education, but age had an association with tolerance apart from education. In 1954 and in 1973, the greater the age, the less the tolerance, but age, like education, was more strongly related to tolerance in 1973 than in 1954. When respondents were grouped by age cohorts, all cohorts increased in tolerance. But the youngest cohort, those who were twenty-one to twenty-nine years old in 1954 and forty to forty-eight in 1973, made the greatest gains in the proportion more tolerant, because this generation was the beneficiary of the post–World War II educational boom in this country.

Another trend taking place in post–World War II America was increasing mobility, and part of that movement was a flow of citizens from rural areas to the cities. Some were claiming that this urbanization of American society was leading to a mass society that would homogenize such characteristics as political attitudes, but the evidence in this study does not support such a theory. Urban dwellers were more tolerant than people who lived in rural areas, but considerable differences in levels of tolerance persist even among urbanites. Furthermore, although tolerance increased in all geographical regions of the country, wide disparities in tolerance were found in 1973. The South persists as the least tolerant region, a distinction not explained by age, education, or migration into the South, even though these variables mitigate what appears to be a culturally determined propensity to greater intolerance.

The post–World War II decades have seen accelerated changes in women's opportunities, culminating in the feminist movement. Previous research, including Stouffer's, led us to expect that political tolerance would be greater among men than women, but the magnitude of the difference in 1973 came as a surprise. Men are clearly more tolerant than women, even with relevant controls applied. And even though both men and women have become more tolerant over the past two decades, men have done so more rapidly than women. Most astonishing of all, the greatest differences between men and women occurred not at the lowest levels of education but at the highest, although education and tolerance are positively associated among women and men.

Still another major theme of the post–World War II era was the so-called secularization of society, a component of modernization said to have reduced the importance of religion. We found little evidence that God could be pronounced dead in modern America, although the crudest indicators of religiosity, affiliation and attendance, showed some signs of decay between 1954 and 1973. Nor has religion's strong hold on intolerance weakened. Whereas affiliates of all major faiths have become more tolerant of nonconformists, those without a religious affiliation have made markedly greater strides toward tolerance. Moreover, church or synagogue attendance is negatively related to tolerance. The more often one attends religious services, regardless of affiliation, the less tolerance one has for nonconformists, including atheists. Nevertheless, a majority of religiously active Americans were willing to let an atheist speak in their communities.

Unfortunately, much of the research on religion and tolerance stops at this point, with at least the intimation that religious people persist as a large segment of the population possessed by bigotry. In our analysis we tried to go a little deeper into religious beliefs and the social-psychological dynamics of intolerance. With some rather dramatic results we observed how some people, finding themselves in a sociocultural context that rendered them powerless and ill-equipped to understand the complexities of the larger world, sought some meaningful explanation of events. These circumstances and the availability of religious interpretations may lead to a world view that personalizes evil and finds confirmation of the Devil's work in social deviants. The unusually strong association of degree of certainty about the Devil's existence and intolerance leaves little doubt about the close link between some religious beliefs and intolerance of social deviants. Religion, particularly in the form of religious ideology, still has a powerful association with the kinds of political attitudes explored in this study. It is an association that for many retards the growth of the kind of civility required in modern society, but much of this segment of the population has had little access to mainstream society and hence little recourse to more sophisticated interpretations of the modern world.

Turning our focus from those who have only limited social and economic resources in society to those who have a greater command of these resources, the socially and politically active citizens, we found that it was indeed those Americans who occupied leadership positions and those who were the most actively involved in community and national life who were the backbone of support for civil liberties. Community leaders, who were not unique in the origins of their tolerance, had much greater levels of commitment to civil liberties than did the general public. However, the gap between leaders and the general public has become smaller in the past two decades. The data also showed that the informed and politically active citizens were most likely to be tolerant. Systematically, those citizens who followed the news more closely; had a greater interest in politics (especially national politics); were opinion leaders among their friends; and actively participated in nonreligious, voluntary associations were more tolerant than those who reported less activism in these areas.

The post–World War II decades, as we have seen, brought revolutionary changes in American society. Changes of such magnitude bring with them social disruption, value confusion, uncertainties, and other strains on the social fabric. Both because of the changes and in spite of the strains, Bill of Rights' principles as guidelines for citizen relationships have advanced, not collapsed. More and more Americans, particularly better informed and active citizens, show signs of greater willingness to extend civil liberties even to those who are considered extreme ideological nonconformists.

The most important descriptive finding of this study was that the majority of rank-and-file Americans scored as more tolerant. Although attitudes and actions are not perfectly correlated, attitudes are important as predispositions to actions, and the social climate of attitudes can be critical in defining appropriate social action. It is for these reasons that the evidence presented in the preceding pages of this book represents important social data. If these facts are known and accepted by most Americans, including their leaders, violations of others' civil liberties, by rank-and-file citizens or political leaders, will not be so easy as in the past. Value commitment can breed social support, and social support makes value commitment more likely. But in the absence of broad public knowledge that such social support exists, vigilante citizens or demagogic leaders find it easier to exploit this "pluralistic ignorance," as social scientists have labeled it.

Evidence of pluralistic ignorance was recently found in a Detroit-area study by Fields and Schuman (1976–1977) and replicated by O'Gorman and Garry (1976–1977) in a national sample. Fields and Schuman included a question comparable to our question about tolerance of atheists. They found that those least tolerant greatly overestimated the percent of people in Detroit who agreed with them, while the most tolerant were much less likely to perceive that others agreed with them.

Americans' tolerance and the potential impact of pluralistic ignorance was recently brought close to home with the controversy over homosexuals' rights and liberties. The Dade County, Florida, vote to repeal an ordinance that banned discrimination against homosexuals in employment, housing, and public accommodations received nationwide attention. There was a great deal of talk, particularly in the news media, that the Dade County controversy might sweep across the nation. Evidence from our study, including data collected several months before the Dade County vote, indicates that such expectations were exaggerated, perhaps as a consequence of the pluralistic ignorance that underestimates the general level of tolerance which exists in the United States. Yet the controversy has not completely disappeared. Without a greater effort to inform the public and leaders of the kind of evidence presented in this study, the conservative bias of pluralistic ignorance might erode even the latent willingness of the majority of Americans to be fair-minded and respectful of homosexuals' civil liberties.

The more democratic a society is, the more that society depends on an informed citizenry. Citizens must want to be informed, but the equation is incomplete without readily accessible, accurate information. Both the unwillingness to be fully informed and the unavailability of credible information can lead to distorted and devious means of obtaining information, such as rumor or reliance on news media and opinion polls that abdicate their responsibility to present full and accurate information. The survey data presented here were gathered and analyzed in a manner that maximized objectivity and accuracy. The sum of the evidence tells us that there is a large reservoir of tolerance in America that includes greater civil liberties for homosexuals. But without wide dissemination of such information, even a tolerant public becomes vulnerable to slanted information sources and demagogic leaders.

Devious information-gathering means are not uncommon among governments either, as the wiretapping of the Watergate era so frightfully reminded us. Nor has wiretapping ended with Watergate. Some efforts to control government spying on citizens have been made, but at the time of this writing, Congress was still debating whether or not to permit wiretapping of citizens without showing that criminal activity was involved. On this issue, the voice of Americans, as represented in this study, is once again loudly and clearly opposed to government wiretapping in general. Indeed, the dramatic shift toward disapproval occurred when the Watergate wiretapping had been publicly disclosed and has persisted at the same high level through 1977, the time of the last measurement.

Rarely have Americans formed such a strong consensus against a political practice relying on national security needs for its justification. Is this finding a sign of greater citizen consciousness and concern for infringements on individual freedoms? Or, to put it another way, are Americans becoming more aware that their own freedoms do not automatically flow from well-intended government policy or from some predestined, collective climate of tolerance? In our study, the empirical linkage between the extent to which citizens felt more or less personal freedom to speak their minds and their willingness to extend civil liberties to others suggests that there is a firm consciousness that one's own freedoms are closely tied to others' freedoms.

Although questions may remain about the depth and durability of these new commitments to civil liberties, the findings of this study indicate a greater awareness on the part of the American people that individual and collective welfare, at least with respect to civil liberties, cannot be taken for granted. Given such an awareness, government leaders may find it increasingly difficult to achieve public support for policies that even subtly permit violations of citizens' liberties.

Our study of community leadership found that leaders were highly tolerant and pluralistic in composition. Yet we rarely hear of leaders, local or national, speaking strongly in favor of constitutional liberties or instructing their constituency on the fragility of those freedoms. More than patriotic, self-aggrandizing lip service to the Bill of Rights is required. Leaders, for example, could capitalize on specific current events, such as a criminal court case, to educate people in the importance of the accused's rights.

Periodic soundings of both the general public's and leaders' commitments to civil liberties should be an essential social indicator of the quality of democratic life in our society. The indications of support for civil liberties presented in this study showed that there is considerable room for improvement in citizen understanding and appreciation of the principles of the Bill of Rights. One common confusion, for example, is the tendency to equate approval of actions with tolerance. This confusion is symptomatic of a deeper misunderstanding of civil liberties that further research and education could greatly reduce. Additional and more periodic checks on levels and sources of commitment would give an informed base on which to build new ways to make civil liberties alive and vital to every citizen.

New ways of encouraging understanding of civil liberties

among school-age youth particularly need to be developed. There is something going on in our schools that promotes tolerance, as our study data consistently showed, but recent studies by the National Assessment of Educational Progress (1972), a project of the Educational Commission of the States, revealed great gaps in knowledge of civil liberties. Among thirteen-year olds, for instance, 81 percent stated that a jury, trial, judge, or court decided whether or not a person is guilty, while only 21 percent believed that a person on radio or television should be allowed to say that Russia is better than the United States.

Schools further tolerance, but we know relatively little about how school environments do so or why understanding of civil libertarian principles is so sketchy. How much effect exposure to new ideas, teachers, peers, general knowledge, civic knowledge, and a host of other educational experiences have on political tolerance and under what conditions they have an effect are still largely unknown.

The effects of diversity are two-sided. Diversity of people can be a valuable resource to a democratic society, or it can generate social strife. Which effect endures depends to a great extent on how well schools prepare the successive generations for the civility that the heterogeneous society requires. In this sense alone, education bears a heavy burden. Yet the 1970s have seen a resurgence of the short-sighted and narrow view of schools as preeminently places to train for occupational roles. Learning to be an accountant will be of little social value if the person is unprepared to live in a pluralistic world that will increasingly demand commingling of people.

Much in this study of American commitment to civil liberties should be encouraging to those who hope for a more civil society. Some findings, however, remind us that there are still many potholes on the road to greater commitment to civil liberties. Indeed, education, the institution that our study showed to be a bulwark in building a tolerant society, may be threatened by one of the most serious strains in American civil libertarianism. Education is a key source of tolerance, but it is in the area of academic freedom that Americans are most restrictive. In our study rarely did a majority support civil liberties for nonconformist college professors, and the trend since 1974 has been toward a slight decline in support for academic freedom.

There are other danger signals in our study that should be

watched carefully if we want to expand tolerance and abate any threat to the progress made. Consistently we found that a hard-core, significant minority of people do not support civil liberties as measured here. There was only a small decline of 3 percent between 1954 and 1973 among those less tolerant. We found a rising percentage of people who believe in the Devil, a belief strongly linked to denying civil liberties to nonconformists.

Troubled times seem to activate these particular religious world views, but societal threat can also weaken the commitment of some of the most tolerant. Hence, threats that arouse fears maintain the potential of eroding tolerance levels, and this should serve to remind us that tolerance, no matter how pervasive, is not maintained as a steady state.

Social change usually brings threats to society with it. And few would quarrel with the claim that we are now living in times of immense change, transition, complexity, and uncertainty—very little has gone unchallenged. Such an environment brings pressures for greater conformity and for constricting tolerance. A return to the stable state, a longing for the clear and simple definition of life, and an ardent defense of tradition have great appeal. On the other hand, change can exert force toward greater flexibility, innovation, and openness to new options. We have seen in this two-decade study that the latter effects seem to have prevailed, but the more constricting effects have by no means disappeared.

The limitations of our measures of support for civil liberties can also serve to make us a little less sanguine about the climate of tolerance in a rapidly changing society. We stated from the start that even though we have strong confidence in our measures, they were basically tapping a predisposition to extend the right to freedom of speech, freedom of the press, and other civil liberties even to those with whom one disagrees. We believe our data show that those most tolerant by our measures are typically those who could be called committed. However, we do not fully know the depth or philosophical basis of their commitment. Are the tolerant, for instance, those who value diversity, or are they, for the most part, merely conforming to respectable norms? And what about the moderately tolerant—if less conducive conditions for expression of tolerance emerged, would they easily shift toward intolerance?

Our conclusion that American commitment to civil liberties shows compelling signs of vitality should be tempered by the limits of our data and by the abiding reality that commitment to the principles of the Bill of Rights is not a static achievement but a process requiring continuous vigilance, effort, and exploration by citizens in a social structure that encourages such commitment. Yet the overall consistency of findings in our study makes it difficult to be pessimistic about the chance for a humane and civil society. The data presented in these chapters give us reason to believe that there is now an emerging American citizenry that will be better prepared to relate to each other with civility in coping with the demanding problems confronting us all.

Research Instruments, Samples, Data Collection, and Methods of Analysis

/\

This appendix provides brief discussions about Stouffer's Scale of Willingness to Tolerate Nonconformists (the primary method of measuring tolerance in his study and ours), the sample designs and their representativeness, interviewer training, and the interviewing experience. These discussions will assist the reader's understanding of the study, its reliability, and its validity. Note, however, that the professional who may wish to use the data collected for this study, when it becomes part of the public domain, or to replicate all or portions of this research should examine the more detailed *Methodological Report for a Study of Tolerance and Political Ideology,* prepared by Response Analysis of Princeton, New Jersey, in December 1973. This report, which includes a copy of the interview schedule, is available on request from the authors.

Stouffer's Scale of Willingness to Tolerate Nonconformists

Stouffer used fifteen items from his interview schedule to measure willingness to tolerate nonconformists. The scale is designed to measure acceptance of behavior even when it is disapproved of. Questions were asked about four types of nonconformists: a Communist, an atheist, a Socialist, and a man whose loyalty has been questioned before a Congressional committee but who swears under oath he has never been a Communist. For each type of nonconformist, questions were asked about such things as whether he should be allowed to keep his job, whether he should be allowed to make a speech in the community, and whether one of his books should be removed from the public library.

The Tolerance Scale is a modified version of a Guttman scale. Guttman scales are designed so that an individual's responses to the items making up the scale should be reproducible from knowing the overall scale score. In developing his scale, Stouffer used a two-step procedure. The first step was a special procedure known as the H or Harvard technique, which involved grouping the fifteen questions into five subsets of three questions each. For a respondent to receive a score point for a subset, it was necessary for the respondent to give a tolerant response to at least two of the three questions. Since the probability of response patterns not fitting the model of a Guttman scale increases with the number of items or questions used, this reduction procedure (reducing the number of items from fifteen to five "contrived" ones) increases the chances of duplicating the perfect scale model. An alternative to the H technique would be to simply choose the five questions that most closely approximate a perfect scale. However, the H technique has an important advantage: Since the five subsets incorporate all fifteen questions, more information is retained in the scale.

In his second step, Stouffer ranked the subsets according to the percentage of respondents receiving point scores. This is comparable to ranking words by spelling difficulty or ranking attitudinal statements by their degree of acceptability to a population. By ranking the subsets of questions, one should be able to reproduce a person's response pattern by knowing the scale score.

The following subsets are the ones used by Stouffer. They are ranked according to the procedure discussed above.

Subset 5. (The most tolerant of all. Make + answers to at least two out of three of these items.)

"Now, I should like to ask you some questions about a man who admits he is a Communist. Suppose this admitted Communist wants to make a speech in your community. Should he be allowed to speak or not?"

+   Yes
—   No
—   Don't know

"Suppose he wrote a book which is in your public library. Somebody in your community suggests the book should be removed from the library. Would you favor removing it, or not?"

—   Favor
+   Not favor
—   Don't know

"Suppose this admitted Communist is a radio (TV) singer (entertainer). Should he be fired, or not?"

—   Should be fired
+   Not be fired
—   Don't know

Subset 4. (The next most tolerant. Fail to qualify in Subset 5 but make + answers to at least two out of three of the following.)

"Should an admitted Communist be put in jail, or not?"

—   Yes
+   No
—   Don't know

"There are always some people whose ideas are considered bad or dangerous by other people. For instance, somebody who is against all churches and religion. If such a person wanted to make a speech in your city (town, community) against churches and religion, should he be allowed to speak, or not?"

+ Yes
— No
— Don't know

"If some people in your community suggested that a book he wrote against churches and religion should be taken out of your public library, would you favor removing this book, or not?"

— Yes
+ No
— Don't know

Subset 3. (Fail to qualify in Subsets 5 and 4, but make + answers to at least two out of three of the following.)

"Now suppose the radio (TV) program he [an admitted Communist] is on advertises a brand of soap. Somebody in your community suggests you stop buying that soap. Would you stop, or not?"

— Would stop
+ Would not stop
— Don't know

"Or consider a person who favored government ownership of all the railroads and all big industries. If this person wanted to make a speech in your community favoring government ownership of all the railroads and big industries, should he be allowed to speak, or not?"

+ Yes
— No
— Don't know

"If some people in your community suggested that a book he wrote favoring government ownership should be taken out of your public library, would you favor removing the book, or not?"

— Yes
+ No
— Don't know

Subset 2. (Fail to qualify in Subsets 5, 4, or 3, but make +
answers to at least two out of three of the following.)
"Now I would like you to think of another person. A man
whose loyalty has been questioned before a Congressional committee,
but who swears under oath he has never been a Communist. Suppose
he is teaching in a college or university. Should he be fired, or not?"

— Yes
+ No
— Don't know

"Should he be allowed to make a speech in your community,
or not?"

+ Yes
— No
— Don't know

"Suppose this man is a high school teacher. Should he be fired,
or not?"

— Yes
+ No
— Don't know

Subset 1. (The next to least tolerant group. Fail to qualify in
Subsets 5, 4, 3, and 2, but make + answers to two out of three of the following.)
"With respect to a man whose loyalty has been questioned but
who swears he is not a Communist. Suppose he has been working in a
defense plant. Should he be fired, or not?"

— Yes
+ No
+ Don't know

"Suppose he is a clerk in a store. Should he be fired, or not?"

— Yes
+ No
+ Don't know

"Suppose he wrote a book which is in your public library. Somebody in your community suggests the book should be removed from the library. Would you favor removing it, or not?"

— Favor
+ Not favor
. + Don't know

Group 0. (The least tolerant group. Fail to qualify in any of the subsets above.)

Although the scale has a range of 0 to 5, the research findings are most often presented in an attenuated version, using scores of 0 and 1 as "less tolerant," 2 and 3 as "in-between," and 4 and 5 as "most tolerant."

Since neither the items of a given set nor individual responses to them are wholly consistent, it is very important to estimate how well a given scale fits the underlying model of a perfect scale. For Guttman scales there are four statistical procedures that assess the consistency of the scale (that is, how closely it approximates a perfect Guttman scale): the coefficient of reproducibility, the minimum marginal reproducibility, the percent improvement, and the coefficient of scalability. The coefficient of reproducibility measures the extent to which a respondent's scale score is a predictor of his or her response pattern. The coefficient is obtained by dividing the total number of "errors" (response patterns not fitting the Guttman model) by the total number of responses and subtracting the resulting quantity from 1. In general, a good scale should have a coefficient of reproducibility of at least .90. The second measure, the minimum marginal reproducibility, is the smallest coefficient of reproducibility that could have occurred given the percentage of the sample of respondents "approving" (that is, endorsing the items in a given way—in our case, in a tolerant direction). The third measure, the percent improvement, is the difference between the first and second measures. It indicates the extent to which the coefficient of reproducibility is caused by response patterns rather than by the inherent relatedness of the items used in the scale. The final measure, the coefficient of scalability, is an extension of the second and third measures and is obtained by dividing the percent improvement by 1 minus the minimum marginal reproducibility. The resulting coefficient should be at least .60 if the scale is to be considered a reasonable approximation to a perfect Guttman scale.

The results of using these four procedures to estimate the consistency of Stouffer's scale are presented in Table 58.* As can be seen,

Table 58. The Scale of Willingness to Tolerate Nonconformists Meets the Criteria for a Good Scale.

	1954	1973
Coefficient of reproducibility	.90	.90
Minimum marginal reproducibility	.71	.69
Percent improvement	.20	.21
Coefficient of scalability	.68	.66

the necessary criteria for a good scale are met for all the procedures and for both time periods. The similarity of results between 1954 and 1973 demonstrates the reliability of the scale. The validity and generalizability of Stouffer's scale are discussed in Chapter Three.

*Stouffer reported that he obtained a coefficient of reproducibility of .96. At the time when he analyzed his data (1954–55), mechanical data-card sorters were typically used rather than computers. In reevaluating his scale with computer methods and his data, we were unable to replicate the .96 coefficient. Several alternative methods were tried, but none proved successful. Hence, we were forced to conclude that a computational error was made in the original analysis.

Sample Design: The National Cross Section

The Response Analysis national probability sample was used for the general public portion of this study. The rest of the material in this Appendix is an abstracted and slightly modified version of portions of the *Methodological Report* by Response Analysis. Sample locations and households, as well as specific individuals to be interviewed, were specified by the sampling plan and also by explicit instructions to the interviewers. No selection step was left to the discretion of the interviewer.

Probability procedures used for the selection of sample areas, interviewing locations, segments, and housing units were such that, for the national sample, each housing unit in the coterminous United States had the same overall probability of selection.

Primary Sampling Units (PSUs). The entire area of the coterminous United States was first divided into approximately 1,140 PSUs. Each PSU is a well-defined geographic area, usually a county or a group of counties, with a minimum population of 50,000 in 1970. PSUs are of two general types: (1) metropolitan areas or parts of metropolitan areas, and (2) other areas.

Thirty-eight large PSUs were included in the sample as self-representing primary areas. These range in 1970 population size from 1,100,000 to 3,300,000 persons and include the twenty-five largest Standard Metropolitan Statistical Areas (SMSAs) in the United States. All other PSUs were grouped into sixty-five strata, with an average stratum population of approximately 2,000,000 persons in 1970. Within a stratum, PSUs are as much alike as possible in terms of geography, metropolitan or nonmetropolitan areas, population density, and other characteristics. One PSU was selected with probability proportionate to size (1970 population count) from each of the sixty-five strata that included two or more PSUs. The selected PSUs are primary areas in the Response Analysis national sample. Together with the 38 self-representing PSUs, the sample includes a total of 103 primary areas.

Secondary Sampling Units (SSUs). Within the 103 PSUs, 600 SSUs were defined and selected. The SSUs are areas of approximately 2,500 population as of 1970. A SSU may be as small geographically as a block or two in a densely populated portion of a city, or it may be an entire county (or even larger in a sparsely populated rural area). Census microfilm records were used to define and select SSUs. These units were selected with probability proportionate to population.

Of the total 600 SSUs, or interviewing locations, in the sample, 300 were used for the present study. Systematic random procedures were used to select these 300 SSUs.

Selection of Sample Segment in Each Secondary Sampling Unit. Within each of the 300 SSUs, enumeration districts and block groups were divided into sample segments or assignment units. With the use of detailed census maps or other mapping materials, the enumeration districts or block groups were divided into geographic "blocks," using roads, streams, or other distinct boundaries wherever possible. In urbanized areas, Census Block Statistics publications were used to determine the number of housing units in each block. In other areas, where census block counts were not available, interviewers made field counts of housing units, block by block. Probability procedures were used to select one or more blocks or block segments, usually including a total of about twenty-five to forty housing units.

Prelistings of Housing Unit Addresses and Selection of Specific Addresses. In most of the national sample locations, interviewers were assigned to do prelistings of housing unit addresses in the selected sample segments. The prelistings were intended partly to provide close central office control over selection of the final sample of households and partly to permit mailing of a letter in advance of the interviewers' visits to sample households. Prelistings were not assigned to the sixty-eight national sample interviewing locations that were primarily rural "open country" areas, in which listings normally provide descriptions of the housing unit and its location but not addresses that are adequate for postal purposes.

In prelisted locations, the final sample of housing units was randomly selected in the Response Analysis central office. Letters were addressed to sample households and mailed a day or two before interviewers received their assignments. In the sixty-eight locations that were not prelisted, units to be included in the sample were designated by premarked lines on the housing unit listing sheets. Letters were not mailed to these households, but the interviewers did have copies of the letter to take with them. Letters informed the potential respondents that they had been selected through random procedures

as part of a national sample to participate in the study, assured them
that the interview would be completely confidential, and urged their
cooperation.

Selection of Respondent Within Housing Unit. Within each
sample household, interviewers first listed all residents, age eighteen
and over. The listing of eligible persons was made on an interview
face sheet provided for each sample household. Residents eligible for
interview were numbered one to n (n = number of residents age eighteen or over) according to a fixed plan: all males first, oldest to youngest; then females oldest to youngest. A simplified selection table was
provided on the interview face sheet. The person "number" to be
interviewed was assigned in advance according to a systematic random plan.

The plan to interview one person per sample household
"favored" persons living in small households. When there was only
one person age eighteen or over in the household, that person was
automatically included in the sample. When there were two persons
age eighteen and over, each had one chance in two of being included
in the sample, and so on. A weighting system was used to compensate
for this selection system.

Sample Design: Civic Leaders

In one respect, the sample of civic leaders is a purposive rather
than a probability sample. That is, following the original study by
Stouffer, we selected certain types of leaders for study not as representing all community leaders but as representatives of different segments
of a community's population who might be especially relevant with
regard to matters concerning civil liberties. The original study
included the following types of leaders: mayors, school board presidents, library board presidents, chairpeople of the Republican and
Democratic county central committees, Chamber of Commerce presidents, labor union presidents, American Legion commanders,
regents of the DAR, chairpeople of the Community Chest (or United
Fund), Bar Association presidents, newspaper publishers, Women's
Club presidents, and PTA presidents. Because of presumed changes
in influence, the present study replaced regents of the DAR and presidents of the Women's Club with police chiefs and presidents of the

League of Women Voters. It is recognized that certain types of important leaders are not included, such as leaders of religious and minority groups. However, the choices that were made allowed us to compare findings with the original study, and comparability was deemed to be the more important consideration with respect to study objectives.

Sampling Frame. As a sampling frame, we started with the same interviewing locations that had been identified for the national cross section. The objective was to interview leaders in cities with populations between 10,000 and 150,000. This population range corresponds to the city sizes in Stouffer's study. Using the 300 locations as a reference point, we identified 91 cities within the specified population range. Interviewers were assigned in these cities.

Additional Sampling Steps. The fourteen categories of leaders were assigned to one of two groups: Group A—Republican party, Bar Association, newspaper publisher, mayor, Chamber of Commerce, League of Women Voters, library board; or Group B—Democratic party, Community Chest, labor union, school board, PTA, chief of police, American Legion.

The ninety-one eligible cities were located in seventy counties. When only one of the cities was in the county, seven interviews were conducted in that city (that is, Group A or Group B leaders were assigned at random to that city). When two of the ninety-one cities were in the same county, a random assignment of Group A leaders was made to one of these cities and of Group B leaders to the other city. When there were three or more cities within a county, Group A leaders were randomly assigned to one city and Group B leaders to another city. Other eligible cities in the same county were simply assigned seven leader categories, randomly drawn from among the list of all leader types. (Republican and Democratic officials presided over countywide organizations. Thus, the randomly drawn leader assignments for the third or other eligible cities in a county were drawn from among the twelve other types of leaders.)

Of the 91 cities, 7 had two general public interviewing locations, instead of one. In these cities, double the usual number of leader interviews were assigned. This procedure yielded 686 assignments rather than the 637 that would have been assigned with seven leaders being interviewed in each of the 91 cities. After the leadership interviews were underway, 50 more assignments were made to ensure a total sample of 650 leaders. Of these assignments, 649 were completed and able to be analyzed.

Interviewer Training

The study used 277 interviewers, nearly all of whom were present at one-day regional training sessions conducted in twenty-seven cities. Response Analysis professional staff members conducted the training meetings, with about ten interviewers at each session. Following a pretraining conference, the first actual interviewing training session, involving ten interviewers, was held. All the trainers were present at this demonstration session.

A week before coming to the training meeting, each interviewer had been sent a copy of the questionnaire with instructions to complete a practice interview and to bring the questionnaire to the meeting. The practice interview, plus a manual prepared for the study, were the resource documents used at the meetings. The agenda for training meetings included the following:

- Interviewers filled out portions of the questionnaire, responding with their own attitudes.
- Nature and purpose of the study, and orientation to our goals.
- Detailed discussion of the questionnaire. Practice interviews were used as an aid in discussion of specific questionnaire problems.
- Review of general interviewing procedures.
- The leadership sample, and discussion of the fourteen categories of leaders.
- A further review of sampling procedures, including housing unit listings and selection of specific respondents.
- Administrative matters, such as how to obtain high completion rates, scheduling of call-backs, how to use the introductory letter.

Interviewing Experience

A total of 5,669 households were assigned. Of these, 592 of the housing units were vacant. This left 5,077 units that were occupied and eligible for interview. In all, 396 potential respondents were not at home after four visits, 863 refused to be interviewed, and 263 interviews were not completed for other reasons. Of the 3,555 interviews that were completed, 15 were judged unsatisfactory. Thus, 3,540 interviews were available for analysis. As a validity check, Response Analysis conducted a telephone interview with 587 of the respondents to verify that they were in fact interviewed and that the interviewer had selected the proper respondent in the household.

Overall, the response rate, that is, the percentage of completed interviews from all eligible households, was 69.7 percent. This rate varied slightly by region, with a 67.6 percent completion rate from the North Central portion of the nation to a 72.8 percent completion rate from the South. The response rate from large cities, those with a population of one million or more, was lower, 64.4 percent, than from other urban areas, 72.5 percent, and from nonmetropolitan areas, 74.6 percent.

To account for differences in the completion rate among locations, each location was given a weight factor equal to the number of eligible households divided by the number of completed interviews. In a few cases, two or more locations were combined to avoid giving any individual respondent an excessively high weight. In addition, as mentioned, households were weighted to compensate for the selection procedure that "favored" smaller households.

After carrying out the household and location weighting procedures, demographic characteristics of the weighted sample were compared to the most recent census data available. This comparison showed that there was some oversampling of women, the better educated, and those under sixty-five years of age. Additional weighting was done to compensate for these discrepancies. After this adjustment, a comparison with census data showed a very close approximation with respect to household size; gender of respondent and household head; marital status of respondent and household head; number of children under eighteen years old; respondent's age, ethnicity, and education; and region of residence. The largest difference was 4 percent; the national sample shows 72.1 percent married, and the census shows 68.1 percent married.

References

/\

ABERBACK, J. "Alienation and Political Behavior." *American Political Science Review*, 1969, *63*, 86–99.

ALFORD, R., and SCOBLE, H. "Community Leadership, Education, and Political Behavior." *American Sociological Review*, 1968, *33*, 259–271.

ALLPORT, G. W., and ROSS, J. M. "Personal Religious Orientation and Prejudice." *Journal of Personality and Social Psychology*, 1967, *5*, 432–443.

ALMOND, G., and VERBA, S. *The Civic Culture*. Princeton, N.J.: Princeton University Press, 1963.

ALTBACH, P. G., and KELLY, D. H. *American Students*. Lexington, Mass.: Heath, 1973.

ANDREWS, F., and others. *Multiple Classification Analysis*. Ann Arbor: Institute for Social Research, University of Michigan, 1973.

BACHRACH, P. *The Theory of Democratic Elitism*. Boston: Little, Brown, 1967.

BALTES, P. B., and SCHAIE, K. W. "On Life-Space Developmental Research Paradigms: Retrospects and Prospects." In P. B. Baltes and K. W. Schaie (Eds.), *Personality and Socialization*. New York: Academic Press, 1973.

BELL, D. *The Coming of Post-Industrial Society*. New York: Basic Books, 1973.

BELLAH, R. N. "Civil Religion in America." *Daedalus,* 1967, *96,* 1–21.

BENGTSON, V. L. "Generation and Family Effects in Value Socialization." *American Sociological Review,* 1975, *40,* 358–371.

BENGTSON, V. L., and BLACK, K. D. "Intergenerational Relations and Continuities in Socialization." In P. B. Baltes and K. W. Schaie (Eds.), *Personality and Socialization.* New York: Academic Press, 1973.

BENGTSON, V. L., and LAUFER, R. S. "Youth, Generations, and Social Change: Parts I and II." *Journal of Social Issues,* 1974, *30.*

BERELSON, B., LAZARSFELD, P., and MC PHEE, W. *Voting.* Chicago: University of Chicago Press, 1954.

BERGER, B. "How Long Is a Generation?" *British Journal of Sociology,* 1960, *11.* Reprinted in and quoted from Berger, B., *Looking for America.* Englewood Cliffs: Prentice-Hall, 1971.

BERGER, P. *The Noise of Solemn Assemblies.* Garden City, N.Y.: Doubleday, 1961.

BERGER, P. *The Sacred Canopy.* Garden City, N.Y.: Doubleday, 1967.

BERGER, P., BERGER, B., and KELLNER, H. *The Homeless Mind.* New York: Vintage Press, 1974.

BERNARD, J. "Age, Sex, and Feminism." *Annals of the American Academy of Political and Social Sciences,* 1974, *415,* 120–137.

BLAU, P. M. "Parameters of Social Structure." *American Sociological Review,* 1974, *39,* 615–635.

BLUMENTHAL, M. D., and others. *Justifying Violence: Attitudes of American Men.* Ann Arbor: Institute for Social Research, University of Michigan, 1972.

BONARIUS, H. *Response Style Psychology: The Rise and Fall of a Fashion.* Paper presented at the Nebraska Symposium on Motivation, Lincoln, 1975.

BORHEK, J. T. "A Theory of Incongruent Experience." *Pacific Sociological Review,* 1965, *8,* 89–95.

BOUDON, R. *Education, Opportunity, and Social Inequality.* New York: Wiley, 1974.

BUSS, A. R. "Generational Analysis: Description, Explanation, and Theory." *Journal of Social Issues,* 1974, *30,* 55–72.

CAMPBELL, A. "Politics Through the Life Cycle." *The Gerontologist,* 1971, *11,* 112–117.

CAMPBELL, A., and others. *The American Voter.* New York: Wiley, 1960.

CANTRIL, A., and ROLL, C., JR. *Hopes and Fears of the American People.* New York: Potomac Associates, 1971.

COMER, J., and WELCH, S. "A Comparison of Elite and Mass Attitudes in a Local Community: A Test of Two Hypotheses." Paper presented at the annual meeting of the American Political Science Association, San Francisco, 1975.

CONNELL, R. W. "Political Socialization in the American Family: The Evidence Reexamined." *Public Opinion Quarterly,* 1972, *36,* 323–333.

CONVERSE, P. "The Nature of Belief Systems in Mass Publics." In D. Apter (Ed.), *Ideology and Discontent.* New York: Free Press, 1964.

COX, H. *The Secular City.* New York: Macmillan, 1966.

CROCKETT, H. J., JR. "On Political Tolerance: Comments on 'Origins of Tolerance: Findings from a Replication of Stouffer's *Communism, Conformity, and Civil Liberties.*'" *Social Forces,* 1976, *55,* 409–412.

CUTLER, N. P., and BENGTSON, V. L. "Age and Political Alienation: Maturation, Generation, and Period Effects." *Annals of the American Academy of Political and Social Sciences,* 1974, *415,* 160–175.

DAHL, R. *A Preface to Democratic Theory.* Chicago: University of Chicago Press, 1954.

DAHL, R. *Who Governs?* New Haven, Conn.: Yale University Press, 1961.

DEMERATH, N. J., III. *Social Class in American Protestantism.* Chicago: Rand McNally, 1965.

DI PALMA, G., and MC CLOSKY, H. "Personality and Conformity: The Learning of Political Attitudes." *American Political Science Review,* 1970, *64,* 1054–1073.

DITTES, J. E. "Psychology of Religion." In G. Lindzey and E. Aronson (Eds.), *Handbook of Social Psychology.* Vol. 5. Reading, Mass.: Addison-Wesley, 1969.

DOUVAN, E., and GOLD, M. "Modal Patterns in American Adolescence." In L. W. Hoffman and M. L. Hoffman (Eds.), *Review of Child Development Research.* Vol. 2. New York: Russell Sage Foundation, 1966.

DUNCAN, O. D. "Inheritance of Poverty or Inheritance of Race?" In

D. P. Moynihan (Ed.), *On Understanding Poverty*. New York: Basic Books, 1969.

DURKHEIM, E. *Elementary Forms of the Religious Life.* (J. W. Swain, Trans.) London: Allen & Unwin, 1912.

ERBE, W. "Social Involvement and Political Activity: A Replication and Elaboration." *American Sociological Review*, 1964, *29*, 198–215.

ERIKSON, K. T. *Wayward Puritans: A Study in the Sociology of Deviance.* New York: Wiley, 1966.

ERSKINE, H. "The Polls: Pacificism and the Generation Gap." *Public Opinion Quarterly*, 1972–1973, *36*, 616–627.

ETZIONI, A. *The Moon-Doggle.* Garden City, N.Y.: Doubleday, 1964.

ETZIONI, A. *The Active Society.* New York: Free Press, 1968.

ETZIONI, A., and NUNN, C. Z. "The Public Appreciation of Science in Contemporary America." *Daedalus*, 1974, *103*, 191–205.

FELDMAN, K. A., and NEWCOMB, T. M. *The Impact of College on Students.* Vol. 1. San Francisco: Jossey-Bass, 1969.

FERGUSON, C. W. *The Male Attitude.* Boston: Little, Brown, 1966.

FERRAR, J. W. "The Dimensions of Tolerance." *Pacific Sociological Review*, 1976, *19*, 63–81.

FERRISS, A. L. *Indicators of Trends in American Education.* New York: Russell Sage Foundation, 1969.

FIELDS, J. M., and SCHUMAN, H. "Public Beliefs About the Beliefs of the Public." *Public Opinion Quarterly*, 1976–77, *40*, 427–448.

FISCHER, C. S. "A Research Note on Urbanism and Tolerance." *American Journal of Sociology*, 1971, *76*, 847–856.

FISCHER, C. S. "Urbanism as a Way of Life: A Review and an Agenda." *Sociological Methods and Research*, 1972, *1*, 187–242.

FISCHER, C. S. "On Urban Alienations and Anomie: Powerlessness and Social Isolation." *American Sociological Review*, 1973, *38*, 311–326.

FISCHER, C. S. "The Effect of Urban Life on Traditional Values." *Social Forces*, 1975a, *53*, 420–432.

FISCHER, C. S. "Toward a Subcultural Theory of Urbanism." *American Journal of Sociology*, 1975b, *80*, 1319–1341.

FISCHER, E. M. "Change in Anomie in Detroit from the 1950s to 1971." Unpublished doctoral dissertation, University of Michigan, 1974.

FONER, A. "Age Stratification and Age Conflict in Political Life." *American Sociological Review*, 1974, *39*, 187–196.

FRAZIER, N., and SADKER, M. *Sexism in School and Society.* New York: Harper & Row, 1973.

GALBRAITH, J. K. *The Affluent Society.* Boston: Houghton Mifflin, 1958.

GALLUP POLL. *Religion in America: 1975.* Report Number 114. Princeton, N.J.: Gallup Opinion Index, 1975.

GLAZER, N., and LIPSET, S. M. "The Polls on Communism and Conformity." In D. Bell (Ed.), *The New American Right.* New York: Criterion Books, 1955.

GLENN, N. D. "Massification Versus Differentiation: Some Trend Data from National Surveys." *Social Forces,* 1967, *46,* 172–180.

GLENN, N. D. "Aging and Conservatism." *Annals of the American Academy of Political and Social Sciences,* 1974, *415,* 176–186.

GLENN, N. D., and ALSTON, J. P. "Rural-Urban Differences in Reported Attitudes and Behavior." *Southwestern Social Science Quarterly,* 1967, *47,* 381–400.

GLENN, N. D., and SIMMONS, J. L. "Are Regional Cultural Differences Diminishing?" *Public Opinion Quarterly,* 1967, *31,* 176–193.

GLOCK, C. Y., and STARK, R. *Religion and Society in Tension.* Chicago: Rand McNally, 1965.

GLOCK, C. Y., and STARK, R. *Christian Beliefs and Anti-Semitism.* New York: Harper & Row, 1966.

GOLDMAN, E. *The Crucial Decade: 1945–1960—and After.* New York: Vintage Books, 1960.

GREELEY, A. *Unsecular Man.* New York: Schocken Books, 1972.

HACKNEY, S. "Southern Violence." *American Historical Review,* 1969, *74,* 906–925.

HADDEN, J. K. *The Gathering Storm in the Churches.* Garden City, N.Y.: Doubleday, 1969.

HAMILTON, C. H. "Continuity and Change in Southern Migration." In J. C. McKinney and E. T. Thompson (Eds.), *The South in Continuity and Change.* Durham, N.C.: Duke University Press, 1965.

HARRIS, L. *Confidence and Concern: Citizens View American Government.* Washington, D.C.: U.S. Government Printing Office, 1973.

HAUSER, P. M. "The Chaotic Society: Product of the Social Morphological Revolution." *American Sociological Review,* 1969, *34,* 1–19.

HENTOFF, N. "If You Liked '1984,' You'll Love 1973." *Playboy,* 1973, *20,* 147ff.

HILL, s. s., JR. *The Southern Church in Crisis.* Boston: Beacon Press, 1968.

HOFSTADTER, R. *The Paranoid Style in American Politics and Other Essays.* New York: Knopf, 1965.

HOGE, D. R., and CARROLL, J. J. "Religiosity and Prejudice in Northern and Southern Churches." *Journal for the Scientific Study of Religion,* 1973, *12,* 181–197.

HOGE, D. R., and CARROLL, J. J. "Christian Beliefs, Nonreligious Factors, and Anti-Semitism." *Social Forces,* 1975, *53,* 581–584.

HYMAN, H. H. "England and America: Climates of Tolerance and Intolerance." In D. Bell (Ed.), *The Radical Right.* Garden City, N.Y.: Doubleday, 1963.

HYMAN, H. H., WRIGHT, C. R., and REED, J. S. *The Enduring Effects of Education.* Chicago: University of Chicago Press, 1975.

INBAU, F., and CARRINGTON, F. "The Case for the So-Called 'Hard Line' Approach to Crime." *Annals of the American Academy of Political and Social Sciences,* 1971, *397,* 19–27.

INGLEHART, R. "The Silent Revolution in Europe: Intergenerational Change in Post-Industrial Societies." *American Political Science Review,* 1971, *65,* 991–1017.

INKELES, A., and SMITH, D. *Becoming Modern.* Cambridge, Mass.: Harvard University Press, 1974.

JACKMAN, M. R. "Political Elites, Mass Publics, and Support for Democratic Principles." *Journal of Politics,* 1972, *34,* 753–773.

JACKMAN, M. R. "Education and Prejudice or Education and Response-Set?" *American Sociological Review,* 1973, *38,* 327–339.

JACKMAN, R. "Much Ado About Nothing." *Journal of Politics,* 1977, *39,* 185–192.

JENCKS, C., and others. *Inequality.* New York: Basic Books, 1972.

JOHNSON, B. "Do Holiness Sects Socialize in Dominant Values?" *Social Forces,* 1961, *39,* 309–316.

KARLSSON, G., and CARLSSON, K. "Age, Cohorts, and the Generation of Generations." *American Sociological Review,* 1970, *35,* 710–718.

KATZ, D. "Factors Affecting Social Change: A Social-Psychological Interpretation." *Journal of Social Issues,* 1974, *30,* 159–180.

KELMAN, H. C. "Compliance, Identification, and Internalization:

Three Processes of Opinion Change." *Journal of Conflict Resolution*, 1958, *2*, 51–60.

KEY, V. O. *Public Opinion and American Democracy*. New York: Knopf, 1961.

KOHN, M. L. *Class and Conformity: A Study in Values*. Homewood, Ill.: Dorsey Press, 1969.

KORNHAUSER, W. *The Politics of Mass Society*. New York: Free Press, 1959.

KORNHAUSER, W. " 'Power Elite' or 'Veto Groups'?" In R. Bendix and S. M. Lipset (Eds.), *Class, Status, and Power*. New York: Free Press, 1966.

LAMBERT, T. A. "Generations and Change: Toward a Theory of Generations as a Force in Historical Process." *Youth and Society*, 1972, *4*, 21–46.

LAZARSFELD, P., and THIELENS, W., JR. *The Academic Mind*. New York: Free Press, 1958.

LAZERWITZ, B. "Religion and Social Structure in the United States." In L. Schneider (Ed.), *Religion, Culture, and Society*. New York: Wiley, 1964.

LENSKI, G. *The Religious Factor*. Garden City, N.Y.: Doubleday, 1963.

LIPPMANN, W. "The Indispensable Opposition." In H. S. Commager (Ed.), *Living Ideas in America*. New York: Harper & Row, 1951.

LIPSET, S. M. "Some Social Requisites of Democracy." *American Political Science Review*, 1959, *53*, 69–105.

LIPSET, S. M. *Political Man*. Garden City, N.Y.: Doubleday, 1960.

LIPSET, S. M. "Religion in the American Past and Present." In R. Lee and M. E. Marty (Eds.), *Religion and Social Conflict*. New York: Oxford University Press, 1964.

LIPSET, S. M., and RAAB, E. *The Politics of Unreason: Right-Wing Extremism in America: 1790–1970*. New York: Harper & Row, 1970.

LIPSET, S. M., TROW, M., and COLEMAN, J. *Union Democracy*. New York: Free Press, 1956.

MC CLOSKY, H. "Consensus and Ideology in American Politics." *American Political Science Review*, 1964, *58*, 361–382.

MANNHEIM, K. "The Problem of Generations." In P. Kecskemeti (Ed.), *Essays on the Sociology of Knowledge*. Boston: Routledge & Kegan Paul, 1964.

MARCUSE, H. "Repressive Tolerance." In R. P. Wolff, B. Moore, Jr., and H. Marcuse (Eds.), *A Critique of Pure Tolerance.* Boston: Beacon Press, 1965.

MEAD, M. *Male and Female.* New York: William Morrow, 1949.

MIDDLETON, R. "Do Christian Beliefs Cause Anti-Semitism?" *American Sociological Review,* 1973, *38,* 33–52.

MIDDLETON, R. "Regional Differences in Prejudice." *American Sociological Review,* 1976, *41,* 94–117.

MILBRATH, L. *Political Participation.* Chicago: Rand McNally, 1965.

MILLER, S. M., and ROBY, P. A. *The Future of Inequality.* New York: Basic Books, 1970.

MILLS, C. W. *The Power Elite.* New York: Oxford University Press, 1956.

MORISON, S. E. *The Oxford History of the American People.* Vol. 3. New York: New American Library, 1972.

NATIONAL ASSESSMENT OF EDUCATIONAL PROGRESS. *National Assessment Report 9: Citizenship.* Washington, D.C.: U.S. Government Printing Office, May 1972.

NELSEN, H. N., and YOKLEY, R. L. "Civil Rights Attitudes of Rural and Urban Presbyterians." *Rural Sociology,* 1970, *35,* 161–174.

NEUGARTEN, B. L. "Age Groups in American Society and the Rise of the Young-Old." *Annals of the American Academy of Political and Social Sciences,* 1974, *415,* 187–198.

NEVINS, A. *The March of Democracy.* New York: Scribner's, 1955.

NEW YORK TIMES. "The Presidential Issue." October 22, 1972, p. 12.

NEW YORK TIMES. September 13, 1976a.

NEW YORK TIMES. March 30, 1976b.

NUNN, C. Z. "Support of Civil Liberties Among College Students." *Social Problems,* 1973, *20,* 300–310.

NUNN, C. Z. "The Rising Credibility of the Devil." *Listening: Journal of Religion and Culture,* 1974, *9,* 84–100.

O'GORMAN, H. J., and GARRY, S. L. "Pluralistic Ignorance—A Replication and Extension." *Public Opinion Quarterly,* 1976–77, *40,* 449–458.

PATEMAN, C. *Participation and Democratic Theory.* New York: Cambridge University Press, 1970.

PETTIGREW, T. F. "Parallel and Distinctive Changes in Anti-Semitic and Anti-Negro Attitudes." In C. H. Stember (Ed.),

Jews in the Mind of America. New York: Basic Books, 1966.

PHILLIPS, D. L. *Knowledge from What?* Chicago: Rand McNally, 1971.

PLOCH, D. "Religion as an Independent Variable: A Critique of Some Major Research." In A. W. Eister (Ed.), *Changing Perspectives in the Scientific Study of Religion.* New York: Wiley, 1974.

PRESSER, S., and SCHUMAN, H. "Question Wording as an Independent Variable in Survey Analysis: A First Report." Paper presented at the American Statistical Association meetings, Atlanta, August 1975.

PROTHRO, J. W., and GRIGG, C. M. "Fundamental Principles of Democracy: Bases of Agreement and Disagreement." *Journal of Politics,* 1960, *22,* 276–294.

PRUYSER, P. W. *Between Belief and Unbelief.* New York: Harper & Row, 1974.

REED, J. S. *The Enduring South.* Lexington, Mass.: Heath, 1972.

RIESMAN, D. *The Lonely Crowd.* New Haven, Conn.: Yale University Press, 1950.

ROKEACH, M. *The Open and Closed Mind.* New York: Basic Books, 1960.

ROSE, A. *The Power Structure.* New York: Oxford University Press, 1967.

ROSEN, B. C., CROCKETT, H. J., JR., and NUNN, C. Z. (Eds.). *Achievement in American Society.* Cambridge, Mass.: Schenkman, 1969.

RYDER, N. B. "The Cohort as a Concept in the Study of Social Change." *American Sociological Review,* 1965, *30,* 843–861.

ST. PETER, L., WILLIAMS, J. A., JR., and JOHNSON, D. R. "Comments on Jackman's 'Political Elites, Mass Publics, and Support for Democratic Principles.'" *Journal of Politics,* 1977, *39,* 176–184.

SALLACH, D., BABCHUK, N., and BOOTH, A. "Social Involvement and Political Activity: Another View." *Social Science Quarterly,* 1972, *52,* 879–892.

SCHAIE, K. W. "A General Model for the Study of Developmental Problems." *Psychological Bulletin,* 1965, *64,* 92–107.

SCHAIE, K. W., and STROTHER, C. R. "A Cross-Sequential Study of Age Changes in Cognitive Behavior." *Psychological Bulletin,* 1968, *70,* 671–680.

SCHWARTZ, M. A. *Trends in White Attitudes Toward Negroes.*

Chicago: National Opinion Research Center, University of Chicago, 1967.

SELZNICK, G. J., and STEINBERG, S. *The Tenacity of Prejudice.* New York: Harper & Row, 1969.

SHILS, E. "The Theory of Mass Society." In P. Olson (Ed.), *America as a Mass Society.* New York: Free Press, 1962.

SHILS, E. "Dreams of Plenitude, Nightmares of Scarcity." In S. M. Lipset and P. G. Altbach (Eds.), *Students in Revolt.* Boston: Houghton Mifflin, 1969.

SNIDERMAN, P. M. *Personality and Democratic Politics.* Berkeley: University of California Press, 1975.

SPILKA, B. "Research on Religious Beliefs: A Critical Review." In M. D. Strommen (Ed.), *Research on Religious Development.* New York: Hawthorn, 1971.

STARK, R., and GLOCK, C. Y. *American Piety: The Nature of Religious Commitment.* Berkeley: University of California Press, 1968.

STEINBECK, J. *The Grapes of Wrath.* New York: Viking Press, 1967. (Originally published 1939.)

STEMBER, C. H. *Education and Attitude Change.* New York: Institute of Human Relations Press, 1961.

STOUFFER, S. A. *Communism, Conformity, and Civil Liberties.* Garden City, N.Y.: Doubleday, 1955.

STROMMEN, M. P., and others. *A Study of Generations.* Minneapolis: Augsburg, 1972.

Sunday Journal and Star (Lincoln, Neb.), August 10, 1975, p. 1.

SWANSON, G. E. *The Birth of the Gods.* Ann Arbor: University of Michigan Press, 1960.

TROW, M. "Small Businessmen, Political Tolerance, and Support for McCarthy." *American Journal of Sociology,* 1958, *54,* 270–281.

TROW, M. "The Second Transformation of American Secondary Education." In R. Bendix and S. M. Lipset (Eds.), *Class, Status, and Power.* (2nd ed.) New York: Free Press, 1966.

U.S. BUREAU OF THE CENSUS. *Statistical Abstract of the United States: 1974.* (95th ed.) Washington, D.C.: U.S. Government Printing Office, 1974.

U.S. BUREAU OF THE CENSUS. *Statistical Abstract of the United States:*

1975. (96th ed.) Washington, D.C.: U.S. Government Printing Office, 1975.

U.S. COMMISSION ON POPULATION GROWTH AND THE AMERICAN FUTURE. *Population and the American Future.* New York: Signet, 1972.

U.S., CONGRESS, SENATE, SUBCOMMITTEE ON CONSTITUTIONAL RIGHTS OF THE SENATE COMMITTEE ON THE JUDICIARY. *Congressional Digest,* 1971, *50,* 233ff.

U.S DEPARTMENT OF JUSTICE. *Report of the Community Relations Service, Student Unrest Survey.* Washington, D.C.: U.S. Government Printing Office, 1969.

U.S. DEPARTMENT OF JUSTICE. *Uniform Crime Reports of the Federal Bureau of Investigation.* Washington, D.C.: U.S. Government Printing Office, annual.

VANCE, R. B. "The Regional Concept as a Tool for Research." In M. Jensen (Ed.), *Regionalism in America.* Madison: University of Wisconsin Press, 1951.

WATTENBERG, B. J. *The Real America.* Garden City, N.Y.: Doubleday, 1974.

WHITT, H. P., and NELSEN, H. N. "Residence, Moral Traditionalism, and Tolerance of Atheists." *Social Forces,* 1975, *54,* 328–340.

WILLETS, F. K., BEALER, R. C., and CRIDER, D. M. "Leveling of Attitudes in Mass Society: Rurality and Traditional Morality in America." *Rural Sociology,* 1973, *38,* 36–45.

WILLIAMS, J. A., JR., NUNN, C. Z., and ST. PETER, L. "Origins of Tolerance: Findings from a Replication of Stouffer's *Communism, Conformity, and Civil Liberties.*" *Social Forces,* 1976a, *55,* 394–408.

WILLIAMS, J. A., JR., NUNN, C. Z., and ST. PETER, L. "Reply to Crockett." *Social Forces,* 1976b, *55,* 413–418.

WILLIAMS, R. M., JR. "Changes in Value Orientations." In C. H. Stember (Ed.), *Jews in the Mind of America.* New York: Basic Books, 1966.

WILSON, W. C. "Extrinsic Religious Values and Prejudice." *Journal of Social Psychology,* 1960, *60,* 286–297.

WIRTH, L. "Urbanism as a Way of Life." *American Journal of Sociology,* 1938, *44,* 8–20.

WOODWARD, C. V. *The Burden of Southern History.* Baton Rouge: Louisiana State University Press, 1968.

YANKELOVICH, D. *The New Morality: A Profile of American Youth in the Seventies.* New York: McGraw-Hill, 1974.

YINGER, J. M. *The Scientific Study of Religion.* New York: Macmillan, 1970.

ZUCKERMAN, H., and COLE, J. R. "Women in American Science." *Minerva,* 1975, *13,* 82–102.

ZURCHER, L. *Poverty Warriors.* Austin: University of Texas Press, 1970.

Index

205